ILLUSTRATED FIRST AID in ENGLISH

Angus Maciver

HODDER
EDUCATION
AN HACHETTE UK COMPANY

Preface

Used wherever the English language is spoken or taught, this book has proved invaluable in class and as a reference book, both to native English speakers and to students of English as a second language.

For all such students *Illustrated First Aid in English* is an essential companion, helpful alike in cases of difficulty with vocabulary, spelling, syntax, idiom and correct usage.

Students of English as a second language have found it of immense value both as an aid to conversation and as a rapid revision course before taking examinations.

A separate answer book is available:

Answers to First Aid in English (ISBN 978 0 340 88288 7)

Orders: please contact Bookpoint Ltd, 130 Milton Park, Abingdon, Oxon OX14 4SB. Telephone: 144 (0)1235 827720. Fax: 144 (0)1235 400454. Lines are open from 9.00 to 5.00, Monday to Saturday, with a 24-hour message answering service. You can also order through our website www.hoddereducation.com

First published 1938 by Hodder Gibson, an Hachette UK company,
Carmelite House, 50 Victoria Embankment, London EC4Y 0DZ
First Aid in English first published 1938
The New First Aid in English first published 1956
The New First Aid in English Revised first published 1986 and
reprinted 19 times
Second edition published 2004
Colour edition published 2013
This Illustrated edition first published 2015

Impression number   10 9 8 7 6 5
Year   2020

Typeset by Baseline Publishing Services

Printed and bound in India.

A CIP catalogue record for this title is available from the British Library

ISBN 978 1 471 85998 4

Contents

The English language

English is an international language. It is written and spoken all over the world. It is spoken in a variety of accents – English, American, West Indian, Indian – but its grammar and most of its vocabulary remain the same no matter where it is used. The English used in a newspaper like Jamaica's *Daily Gleaner* is much the same as the English in *The New York Times*, *The Times of India* or *The Guardian*.

English has borrowed words from almost every other language. Look at these examples:

card (French)   piano (Italian)   fox (German)   bungalow (Hindi)

canoe (Carib)   dictator (Latin)   admiral (Arabic)

English has its origins in northern Europe. Its grammar shows its roots in languages like German and Dutch. A typical English sentence has a noun or noun phrase (subject) followed by a verb and another noun or noun phrase (object), e.g.

The fat man drove a big red car.

[Subject]   [Verb]   [Object]

Parts of speech

English words can be classified into different parts of speech according to the part they play in making sentences in the language. So, all English words fall into eight main categories:

Nouns	A noun is the name of a person, animal, place or thing, e.g. John, tiger, school, kettle, honesty.
Verbs	A verb may be said to be a "doing" word, e.g. eat, think, write.
Pronouns	A pronoun is a word which takes the place of a noun, e.g. he, she, it.
Adjectives	An adjective describes a noun or a pronoun, e.g. good, fine, red.
Adverbs	An adverb generally modifies a verb, e.g. quietly, here, suddenly.
Prepositions	A preposition shows the relation between one thing and another, e.g. against, for, with.
Conjunctions	A conjunction is a word used for joining words and clauses, e.g. and, but.
Exclamations or interjections	An exclamation or interjection expresses sudden emotion, e.g. Oh! Hello! Stop!

When we wish to express a thought, we use words grouped together in a certain order so that we convey a sensible, definite meaning. This combination of words is called a **sentence**. In conversation or writing, sentences should always be used in order that the hearer or reader may clearly understand the meaning.

Number

Most nouns have a **singular** form used to denote **one** person or thing and a different **plural** form denoting **more** than **one**. Pronouns and verbs also have different singular and plural forms.

Singular	Plural
box	boxes
brush	brushes
fox	foxes
gas	gases
glass	glasses
watch	watches
army	armies
city	cities
fly	flies
lady	ladies
calf	calves
half	halves
knife	knives
leaf	leaves
life	lives
loaf	loaves
shelf	shelves
thief	thieves
wolf	wolves
chief	chiefs
dwarf	dwarfs, dwarves
hoof	hoofs, hooves
reef	reefs
roof	roofs
cargo	cargoes
echo	echoes
hero	heroes
wife	wives
potato	potatoes
banjo	banjos

Singular	Plural
day	days
sky	skies
piano	pianos
solo	solos
valley	valleys
child	children
foot	feet
goose	geese
man	men
mouse	mice
ox	oxen
tooth	teeth
woman	women
brother	brothers / brethren
person	people / persons
fish	fishes / fish
genius	geniuses / genii
halo	halos / haloes
penny	pennies / pence

Singular	Plural
cod	cod
deer	deer
dozen	dozen
grouse	grouse
salmon	salmon
sheep	sheep
swine	swine
trout	trout

Singular	Plural
brother-in-law	brothers-in-law
by-way	by-ways
cupful	cupfuls
hanger-on	hangers-on
man-of-war	men-of-war
bye-law	bye-laws
mouse-trap	mouse-traps
passer-by	passers-by
son-in-law	sons-in-law
spoonful	spoonfuls

The following words have no singular:

bellows, billiards, gallows, measles, pincers, pliers, scissors, shears, spectacles, thanks, tidings, tongs, trousers, tweezers, victuals.

Exercises on number

1. State the plural of:
   loaf, man-of-war, piano, sheep, foot, echo, penny, life, deer, ox.

2. Give the singular of:
   ladies, thieves, geese, trout, passers-by, mice, knives, teeth, boxes.

3. Fill in the blank spaces – the singular or plural form – as required:

   army _____   son-in-law _____
   _____ roofs   cargo _____
   _____ women   _____ children
   cupful _____   _____ flies
   swine _____   halo _____
   dwarf _____   _____ potatoes

4. Give the plural of:
   police-constable, daughter-in-law, step-child, looker-on, housewife, fireman.

5. Give the singular of:
   glasses, hoofs, heroes, feet, pence, fish, shelves, cities, men, leaves.

Exercises on number cont.

6. Change all **singulars** into **plurals**.

a) I heard the echo in the cave.

b) The lady spoke to the child.

c) The boy went for a loaf.

d) The man fed the calf.

e) The mouse ran into a hole.

f) The knife was lying on the table.

g) The fisherman caught a trout.

h) The dwarf gave him a stick.

i) The ship struck the reef.

j) My foot troubled me.

k) It was a man's boot.

l) The burglar tried to rob my shop.

m) The prisoner says that he is innocent.

n) The girl's hat was on the peg.

o) The boy robbed a bird's nest.

p) His tooth hurt him badly.

q) The farmer ploughs his field.

r) The horse is eating a raw carrot.

s) The child cried because he was tired.

t) This is the house in which I stay.

7. Change all **singulars** into **plurals** and **verbs** into the **past tense**.

a) The rabbit runs from the dog.

b) The girl wears a blue dress.

c) The sailor swims to his ship.

d) The woman catches the goose.

e) The man shoots the deer.

f) The ox eats the potato.

g) The lady prefers the rose.

h) The sheep runs in the valley.

i) Her foot is badly cut.

j) The thief steals the valuable bag.

k) The child runs to the table.

l) He is a man of means.

m) I keep the bird in a cage.

n) He writes my name.

o) She tells me so.

p) He has a sharp knife.

q) She takes his pencil.

r) The old woman sits on that seat.

s) The man walks slowly to his job.

t) The mouse scampers from the cat.

Gender

Nouns and pronouns belong to one or another of four genders in grammar. These are:

1. **Masculine** – words denoting male creatures, e.g. boy, king.
2. **Feminine** – words denoting female creatures, e.g. girl, queen.
3. **Common** – words denoting creatures of either sex, e.g. child, owner.
4. **Neuter** – words denoting things of neither sex, e.g. house, box.

Masculine	Feminine	Masculine	Feminine
abbot	abbess	bachelor	spinster
actor	actress	beau	belle
baron	baroness	boy	girl
count	countess	bridegroom	bride
duke	duchess	brother	sister
emperor	empress	earl	countess
enchanter	enchantress	father	mother
god	goddess	fiancé	fiancée
heir	heiress	friar	nun
host	hostess	gentleman	lady
lion	lioness	he	she
marquis	marchioness	hero	heroine
master	mistress	him	her
mayor	mayoress	husband	wife
prince	princess	king	queen
male	female	lad	lass
man	woman	lord	lady
monk	nun	masseur	masseuse
nephew	niece	Mr	Mrs
shepherd	shepherdess	sir	madam
sorcerer	sorceress	son	daughter
steward	stewardess	Sultan	Sultana
tiger	tigress	tutor	governess
widower	widow	uncle	aunt
waiter	waitress	wizard	witch

Masculine	Feminine	Masculine	Feminine
boar	sow	billy-goat	nanny-goat
buck	doe	buck-rabbit	doe-rabbit
bull	cow	bull-calf	cow-calf
bullock	heifer	cock-sparrow	hen-sparrow
cock	hen	father-in-law	mother-in-law
colt	filly	grandfather	grandmother
dog	bitch	headmaster	headmistress
drake	duck	he-goat	she-goat
gander	goose	landlord	landlady
hart	hind	male-child	female-child
hound	brach	manservant	maidservant
ram	ewe	postman	postwoman
sire	dam	postmaster	postmistress
stag	hind	son-in-law	daughter-in-law
stallion	mare	stepfather	stepmother
steer	heifer	stepson	stepdaughter
Alexander	Alexandra	John	Joan
Cecil	Cecilia	Joseph	Josephine
Charles	Charlotte	Oliver	Olive
Christian	Christina	Patrick	Patricia
Clarence	Clara	Paul	Pauline
Francis	Frances	Robert	Roberta
George	Georgina	Victor	Victoria
Henry	Henrietta	William	Wilhelmina

Common gender

Common gender words denote creatures of **either sex** and the same word may be used **both of male and of female**, e.g.

adult, animal, baby, bird, cat, cattle, child, companion, comrade, cousin, darling, dear, deer, fowl, friend, guardian, guest, infant, juvenile, orphan, owner, parent, passenger, pig, pupil, relation, relative, scholar, sheep, singer, student, swan, teacher, tourist, traveller, visitor.

Neuter gender

Neuter gender words denote **things without life or sex**, e.g.

bag, boots, box, bread, butter, chair, chalk, chimney, church, cocoa, coffee, desk, dishes, door, floor, house, jacket, jotter, kettle, knife, mirror, pencil, pillow, ruler, school, seat, stairs, street, table.

Exercises on gender

1. Give the feminine of:
   heir, monk, stallion, nephew, gander, waiter, sir, ram, hero, bachelor.

2. Give the masculine of:
   witch, filly, cow, maidservant, wife, duck, bride, duchess, aunt.

3. State the gender of:
   lion, cousin, mistress, friend, pencil, steward, sister, book, child.

4. Give the feminine of:
   headmaster, step-father, son-in-law, billy-goat.

5. Fill in the blank spaces – the masculine or feminine form – as required:

   a) lion _____   f) bull _____

   b) _____ lady   g) grandfather _____

   c) _____ governess   h) _____ hind

   d) male _____   i) _____ widow

   e) actor _____   j) tomcat _____

6. Give the corresponding feminine of:
   Joseph, Henry, Patrick, Charles, John.

Exercises on gender cont.

7. Change all **masculines** into the corresponding **feminines**:
   a) The bridegroom is my nephew.
   b) My landlord is a widower.
   c) The wizard spoke to the prince.
   d) The Duke chatted to the man.
   e) The heir to the estate is a bachelor.
   f) "No, sir," he replied.
   g) The waiter served his own brother.
   h) "He was indeed a hero," said the emperor.
   i) The lion sprang at the colt.
   j) The master gave instructions to the manservant.
   k) "Well!" said his grandfather, "How are you, my little lad?"
   l) The steward brought a glass of water to my uncle, who was seasick.
   m) The host was extremely puzzled by the twin brothers.
   n) The son of a king is called a prince.
   o) The mayor talked to the father of the little boy.
   p) The old man told his shepherd to search for the ram.
   q) His father-in-law spoke to the manager.
   r) He was the stepson of an elderly count.
   s) The headmaster rebuked the boy for his conduct.
   t) He owned a pet gander called Joseph.

Families

A nuclear family refers to just parents and their offspring. An extended family includes grandparents, aunts and uncles, cousins, etc.

Parents		Young
father	mother	baby or child
king	queen	prince or princess
man	woman	baby or child
bear	she-bear	cub
billy-goat	nanny-goat	kid
boar (pig)	sow	piglet
buck (deer)	hind	fawn
buck (hare)	doe	leveret
buck (rabbit)	doe	rack
bull (cattle)	cow	calf
bull (elephant)	cow	calf
bull (seal)	cow	calf
bull (whale)	cow	calf
cob (swan)	pen	cygnet
cock (fowl)	hen	chicken
cock (pigeon)	hen	squab
dog	bitch	pup
dog (fox)	vixen	cub
drake	duck	duckling
eagle	eagle	eaglet
gander	goose	gosling
hawk	bowess	bowet
hold (ferret)	jill	hob
leopard	leopardess	cub
lion	lioness	cub
owl	owl	owlet
ram (sheep)	ewe	lamb
stag (red deer)	hind	fawn
stallion (horse)	mare	foal
tiercel (peregrine)	falcon	eyas
tiger	tigress	cub

	Parents		Young
tomcat	queen or tabby cat		kitten
wolf	she-wolf		cub

Adult	Young		Adult	Young
bee	grub		moth	caterpillar
bird	nestling		salmon	parr
butterfly	caterpillar		toad	tadpole
eel	elver		trout	fry
frog	tadpole		wasp	grub

Exercises on families

1. Name the young of:
   fox, eagle, goose, sheep, pig, goat, cow, horse.

2. Name the parent of:
   fawn, pup, cygnet, chicken, leveret, kitten, owlet, duckling.

3. Fill in the blank spaces – the name of parent or young – as required:

   wolf _____   _____ kid

   _____ foal   bear _____

   sow _____   _____ lamb

   _____ gosling   eagle _____

4. Give the names for:
   a young salmon, a young eel, a young trout, a young bird.

Traditional homes

These days, people live in all sorts of different homes. The lists below refer to traditional homes.

Person	Home		Creature	Home
Aborigine	humpy		badger	sett, earth
convict	prison		bear	den
Inuit	igloo		beaver	lodge
king	palace		bee	hive
lumberjack	log-cabin		bird	nest
Maori	whare		cow	byre, cowshed
minister	manse		dog	kennel
monk	monastery		eagle	eyrie
noble	castle		fowl	coop
Native American	wigwam or tepee		fox	earth, lair
nun	convent		hare	form
parson	parsonage		horse	stable
pioneer	wagon		lion	lair, den
priest (eastern)	temple		mouse	hole, nest
prisoner	cell		pig	sty
soldier	barracks or camp		otter	holt
Swiss (herdsman)	chalet		owl	barn, tree
traveller	caravan		rabbit (tame)	hutch
vicar	vicarage		rabbit (wild)	burrow, warren
Zulu	kraal		sheep	pen, fold
			snail	shell
			spider	web
			squirrel	drey
			tiger	lair
			wasp	nest, vespiary

1. Name the traditional homes of:
    king, minister, lumberjack, parson, monk, Native American, Inuit, Zulu.

2. Whom would you expect to find living in the following?
    convent, palace, barracks, cell, vicarage

3. Name the homes of the following creatures:
    cow, dog, eagle, bee, pig, fox, wild rabbit, wasp, bird, lion.

4. What creatures live in the following places?
    drey, hutch, pen, form, stable

Names

First or Christian or given names: names given to children at their birth, christening, baptism or naming ceremony, usually different for boys and girls. Most have shortened forms – so-called "pet" names or nicknames.

Male first names	Female first names
Abeo	Abigail
Adam	Adimola
Ahmed	Alice
Akiiki	Amanda (Mandy)
Alan	Amy
Alfred (Alf, Fred)	Andrea
Ali	Angela (Angie)
Andrew (Andy, Drew)	Ann (Annie, Nan, Nancy)
Anthony (Tony)	Barbara (Babs)
Antonio	Benita
Ayodele	Bernice
Ben	Caitlin
Brian	Catherine (Cathie, Kate, Kitty)
Carlton	Cecilia (Cis, Cissie)
Charles (Charlie)	Charlotte
Chinwe	Chloe
Christopher (Chris, Kit)	Christina (Chrissie, Tina)
Daniel (Dan, Danny)	Devi
David (Dave)	Doris
Dev	Dorothy (Dot, Dolly)
Edward (Ed, Ned, Ted)	Eleanor (Ella, Ellie, Nell)
Emmanuel	Elizabeth (Betty, Liz, Lizzie)
Errol	Emily
Ethan	Emma
Francis (Frank)	Fiona
Gabriel	Florence (Flo, Flossie)
Garry	Grace
George	Hannah
Gideon	Helen (Nell)
Gordon	Holly
Harry	Jane (Jean, Jeanie)
Hugh (Hughie)	Janet (Jenny, Jess, Jessie)

Male first names	Female first names
Idris	Jessica (Jess)
Jack	Joyce
James (Jamie, Jim, Jimmy)	Judith (Judy)
John (Johnny)	Julia (Julie)
Joseph (Joe, Joey)	Katherine (Kathy, Katie)
Joshua (Josh)	Kim
Kingsly	Lauren
Kintu	Lilian (Lily)
Laurence (Larry)	Lucy
Lewis	Margaret (Marjory, Maggie, Peggy)
Liam	Maria
Luke	Mariam
Malusi	Marion
Marcus	Mary (May, Molly)
Matthew (Matt)	Megan
Michael (Mike, Mick)	Mia
Mohammed	Mina
Nelson	Nina
Oliver	Olivia
Patrick (Pat, Paddy)	Petula
Peter (Pete)	Princess
Philip (Phil)	Promise
Ranjit	Rebecca (Becky)
Ricardo	Rita
Richard (Dick, Richie)	Rose (Rosie)
Robert (Bob, Bobby, Robin, Bert)	Sameera
Samuel (Sam, Sammy)	Sarah (Sally, Sadie)
Shiva	Shanice
Solomon	Sophie
Stephen (Steve)	Susan (Sue, Susie)
Tumelo	Tallulah
Tyrece	Victoria (Vicky)
Uwem	Violet (Vi)
Victor	Winifred
Vishnu	Yasmin
Wesley (Wes)	Yvonne
William (Bill, Will)	Zoë

Where do names come from?

Many first names have a meaning in Hebrew, Greek, Latin, Gaelic or Old English, e.g. Amanda – lovable; Katherine – pure; Charles – manly; Christopher – carrier of Christ; Clement – merciful; Cyril – lordly; Donald – world chief; Ethel – noble; Fiona – fair; Hilary – cheerful; Margaret – pearl; Peter – rock; Philip – lover of horses; Stephen – crown; Zoë – life.

Surnames: a child's last name is usually the family name of the child's father. On marriage a woman normally takes the surname of her husband, though nowadays some do not. Note, however, that in China the surname is not the last, but the first name (see page 21).

Many surnames were formed from:

Occupations	Archer, Baker, Clark, Cook, Farmer, Fisher, Hunter, Mason, Miller, Porter, Shepard, Slater, Smith, Taylor, Wright.
Places	Burns, Cape, England, Forest, Ford, Hall, Hamilton, Hill, Lake, London, Mills, Scotland, Stirling, Wells, Woods.
Animals	Bullock, Fox, Hare, Hart, Hogg, Lamb, Lyon, Wolfe.
Birds	Drake, Nightingale, Peacock, Swan, Wren.
Colours	Black, Blue, Brown, Grey, Green, White.
Qualities of mind or body	Blyth, Bright, Gay, Good, Hardie, Little, Merry, Noble, Short, Small, Smart, Strong, Young.

Names in other countries

In Kenya the word **arap** in a name means "son of", e.g. the former President of Kenya is named Daniel Toroitich arap Moi. Similarly in other districts the Kikuyu, Kamba, Meru and Embu tribes use **wa** meaning "son of" or "daughter of".

In Arabic-speaking countries, parents are often known by their relation to their children. So, Abu means "father of"; Oom means "mother of". So: Abu Ahmed = the father of Ahmed; Oom Ali = the mother of Ali.

In a similar way, children are often known by their relation to their parents by the use of **bin** (son of) and **binte** (daughter of). So: Ahmed bin Fuad = Ahmed, son of Fuad; Faridah binte Hussein = Faridah, daughter of Hussein.

In Singapore, Indian names would include **S/O** (son of) or **D/O** (daughter of), e.g. Selvarajoo S/O Velu or Saraswethy D/O Rajoo.

Chinese names are written with the family name first, e.g. the Prime Minister of Singapore is the Honourable Goh Chok Tong, Goh being the family name.

An interesting fact about Chinese names is that the second name denotes the generation. As an example take the name Tan Wu Cheng. Tan is the family name, Wu the generation name and Cheng the personal name. Should Mr Tan have a brother or brothers they will all bear the same family name, Tan, followed by the generation name Wu followed by their own personal name, Cheng or Ling or any other given name.

In Iceland the boy or girl would, in addition to their own personal name, be given their father's name with the addition of son or daughter, e.g. Magnus' father was called John so Magnus Johnson would be the boy's name.

Group terms or collections

Different names are given to groups or collections of people, birds, animals and objects. Some of these collective names are simply descriptive, others can be quite poetic or imaginative.

Animate

an army of ants	a host of angels	a company of actors	a shoal of herring
an army of soldiers	a litter of cubs	a covey of grouse	a staff of servants
a band of musicians	a litter of pups	a crew of sailors	a staff of teachers
a bench of bishops	a nest of rabbits	a drove of cattle	a stud of horses
a bench of magistrates	a pack of rascals	a flock of birds	a swarm of bees
a board of directors	a pack of wolves	a flock of sheep	a swarm of insects
a brood of chickens	a plague of insects	a gaggle of geese	a team of horses
a building of rooks	a plague of locusts	a gang of labourers	a team of oxen
a choir of singers	a pride of lions	a gang of thieves	a team of players
a class of pupils, students	a school of whales	a group of friends	a troop of monkeys
a herd of cattle		a herd of buffaloes	a troupe of dancers

Inanimate

a bale of cotton, wool

a batch of bread

a bouquet of flowers

a bunch of grapes

a bundle of rags

a chest of drawers

a clump of trees

a cluster of diamonds, stars

a clutch of eggs

a collection of pictures

a crate of fruit

a fleet of cars, ships

a flight of aeroplanes, steps

a forest of trees

a hail of fire

a hedge of bushes

a library of books

a pack of cards

a rope of pearls

a set of china, clubs, tools

a sheaf of corn

a stack of hay

a string of beads

a suit of clothes

a suite of furniture, rooms

a tuft of grass

People

at a concert	audience
in church	congregation
in the street	crowd, throng
in a riot	mob
in a rowdy scene	rabble
at a sporting event	crowd

a baren of mules

a bevy of quails

a cast of hawks

a cete of badgers

a clowder of cats

a covert of coots

a down of hares

a fall of woodcocks

a field of runners

a flight of doves

a flight of swallows

a gang of elks

a gathering of clans

a herd of antelopes

a herd of cranes

a host of sparrows

a kindle of kittens

a labour of moles

a leap of leopards

a muster of peacocks

a nest of mice

a nide of pheasants

a pace of asses

a paddling of ducks

a posse of sheriff's men

a rag of colts

a siege of herons

a skulk of foxes

a sloth of bears

a smuck of jellyfish

a stand of plovers

a string of horses

a tribe of goats

a watch of nightingales

a wisp of snipe

a budget of papers

a bunch of bananas

a cast of flowerpots

a crate of crockery

a fusillade of shots

a galaxy of stars

a group of islands

a nest of machine guns

a peal of bells

a punnet of strawberries

a sheaf of arrows

a shock of wheat

a skein of silk

a skein of wool

a truss of hay

1. A number of sheep together is called a flock. What name is given to a number of:
   singers, ships, wolves, trees, bees, whales, thieves, players, pups?

2. Of what are these collections?
   army, mob, sheaf, bundle, clutch

3. Supply the missing word:
   a) a _____ of cars   f) a _____ of herring
   b) a _____ of servants   g) a _____ of cattle
   c) a _____ of angels   h) a _____ of directors
   d) a _____ of grapes   i) a _____ of chickens
   e) a _____ of monkeys   j) a _____ of books

4. Insert the most suitable word in each of the following:
   a) a litter of _____   f) a cluster of _____
   b) a band of _____   g) a stack of _____
   c) a building of _____   h) a skein of _____
   d) a plague of _____   i) a crew of _____
   e) a bouquet of _____   j) an army of _____

5. Give one word for a number of people:
   a) at a concert   d) in a riot
   b) in church   e) in a rowdy scene
   c) in the street   f) at a football match

6. The following words represent a definite number:
   single, couple, brace, pair, dozen.

   Place the words in the phrases best suited to their use:
   a) a _____ eggs   d) a _____ of boots
   b) a _____ of chairs   e) a _____ ticket
   c) a _____ of grouse

7. At my uncle's farm I saw:
   a) a _____ of sheep   d) a _____ of cattle
   b) a _____ of pups   e) a _____ of chickens
   c) a _____ of bees   f) a _____ of geese

8. Insert the most suitable words in the following sentences:
   a) He was greeted at the station by a _____ of friends.
   b) A _____ of thieves had broken into the premises.
   c) The old shepherd carefully counted his _____ of sheep.
   d) An _____ of ants moved slowly across our path.
   e) The fishermen saw signs of the presence of a _____ of herring.
   f) At the evening service, the minister preached to a large _____.
   g) The attackers were met by a _____ of bullets.
   h) His whole _____ of cattle had been affected by the drought.
   i) The travellers were hotly pursued by a _____ of wolves.
   j) He attended a meeting of the _____ of directors.

9. The following definitions represent **numeral** words; for example, an aeroplane with *one* set of wings is called a **monoplane**.

   How many can you recognise and properly name?
   a) one person singing
   b) a single eye-glass
   c) a fabled animal with one horn
   d) a two-wheeled cycle
   e) a two-footed animal
   f) an aeroplane with two sets of wings
   g) a piece of music written for two performers
   h) two babies born at the same time
   i) a combat between two people
   j) a three-legged stand or support
   k) three people singing together
   l) a three-wheeled cycle
   m) a four-footed animal
   n) four people singing together
   o) a period of ten years
   p) a period of a hundred years
   q) a person aged one hundred years
   r) a Roman commander of one hundred men
   s) creatures said to have one hundred feet

Similes

Similes compare things which are alike in some respect, although they may be different in their general nature.

1. Similes showing distinctive qualities of creatures:

as agile as a monkey
as blind as a bat
as brave as a lion
as bright as a lark
as busy as an ant
as busy as a bee
as calm as a cat
as crafty as a fox
as cunning as a fox
as devoted as a mother
as fast as a deer
as fast as a hare
as fat as a pig
as feeble as a child
as fierce as a lion
as flat as a flounder
as fleet as a gazelle
as frisky as a lamb
as frisky as a two-year-old
as gentle as a dove
as gentle as a lamb
as graceful as a swan

as hairy as a gorilla
as happy as a king
as happy as a lark
as happy as a sandboy
as harmless as a dove
as heavy as an elephant
as hungry as a hunter
as hungry as a wolf
as industrious as a beaver
as like as two herring
as loyal as an apostle
as mad as a hatter
as mad as a March hare
as meek as a lamb
as obstinate as a mule
as old as Methuselah
as patient as Job
as playful as a kitten
as playful as a puppy
as pleased as Punch
as plump as a partridge

More similes showing distinctive qualities of creatures:

as poor as a church mouse

as proud as a peacock

as quiet as a mouse

as red as a turkey-cock

as sick as a dog

as silly as a sheep

as slippery as an eel

as slow as a snail

as slow as a tortoise

as sober as a judge

as stolid as a cow

as strong as a horse

as strong as an ox

as sure-footed as a goat

as swift as a deer

as swift as a hare

as swift as a hawk

as tall as a giant

as tenacious as a bulldog

as tender as a chicken

as tender as a shepherd

as thick as thieves

as timid as a mouse

as timid as a rabbit

as wise as an owl

as wise as Solomon

as white as a ghost

2. Similes showing special qualities of things:

as black as coal
as black as soot
as bold as brass
as bright as a button
as brittle as glass
as brown as a berry
as changeable as the weather
as clean as a whistle
as clear as a bell
as clear as crystal
as cold as charity
as cold as ice
as cool as a cucumber
as dead as a doornail
as deaf as a doorpost
as drunk as a lord
as dry as a bone
as dull as dishwater
as easy as ABC
as easy as winking
as fat as butter
as fit as a fiddle
as flat as a pancake
as fresh as a daisy
as fresh as paint
as good as gold
as green as grass
as hard as iron
as hard as nails
as heavy as lead
as hot as a furnace
as keen as mustard
as large as life
as light as a feather
as alike as two peas

as neat as a new pin
as old as the hills
as open as day
as pale as death
as plain as a pikestaff
as purple as the heather
as quick as lightning
as regular as the clock
as right as rain
as round as a barrel
as round as an orange
as safe as houses
as sharp as a needle
as sharp as a razor
as silent as the grave
as smooth as glass
as smooth as velvet
as soft as butter
as soft as down
as soft as putty
as sound as a bell
as sour as vinegar
as steady as a rock
as stiff as a poker
as straight as an arrow
as straight as a ramrod
as sturdy as an oak
as sweet as honey
as thin as a rake
as tough as leather
as ugly as sin
as warm as wool
as weak as water
as white as a sheet
as white as snow

Exercises on similes

1. We say "as black as coal". Supply the missing words in the following:
   a) as sharp as _____
   b) as keen as _____
   c) as brave as _____
   d) as sweet as _____
   e) as cold as _____
   f) as slippery as _____
   g) as swift as _____
   h) as clear as _____
   i) as light as _____

2. Complete the following:
   a) as _____ as a monkey
   b) as _____ as a flounder
   c) as _____ as Punch
   d) as _____ as a chicken
   e) as _____ as a bee
   f) as _____ as a rock
   g) as _____ as iron
   h) as _____ as a new pin
   i) as _____ as a rabbit
   j) as _____ as the hills

3. Complete the following sentences with suitable words:
   a) The coward was trembling like a _____.
   b) His hands were as cold as _____.
   c) The man could swim like a _____.
   d) The baby was as good as _____.
   e) The boy ran like the _____.

4. Pick out (by underlining) the best simile in the following:
   Example: As dry as (a tree, an egg, <u>a bone</u>, an apple).
   a) As flat as (a kettle, a pancake, a loaf, a saucer).
   b) As steady as (a rock, a book, a box, table).
   c) As fast as (a child, a tortoise, a herring, a deer).
   d) As proud as (a lamb, a daisy, a peacock, a rabbit).
   e) As happy as (a giraffe, a lark, a lobster, a serpent).

5. Add what you consider the most suitable word:
   a) The lake shone like a _____.
   b) The smooth sea was like _____.
   c) The water was as clear as _____.
   d) The boy climbed the tree like a _____.
   e) His terrified companion stuck to him like a _____.

Occupations

An occupation refers to a career or a job, or a form of work.

Describe in a sentence the occupations of the following:

artist	jockey
athlete	joiner
barber	journalist
blacksmith	judge
butcher	lawyer
cabinet-maker	locksmith
caddie	magistrate
caretaker	mason
carpenter	matron
cashier	mechanic
chauffeur	miner
chemist	minister
cleaner	newsagent
clown	nurse
coastguard	optician
cobbler	physician
computer programmer	pilot
conductor	plumber
confectioner	police officer
decorator	porter
dentist	postman/woman
detective	reporter
doctor	sailor
engineer	sculptor
explorer	secretary
farmer	shepherd
florist	shopkeeper
gamekeeper	soldier
glazier	stationer
greengrocer	steeplejack
grocer	surgeon
hairdresser	tailor
ironmonger	teacher

With whom do you associate the following?

anvil	handcuffs	razor	spectacles
awl	harness `	rifle	telescope
barrow	knife	roofs	ticket-punch
baton	lancet	safety lamp	tins
briefcase	mail	saw	tractor
cleaver	palette	scales	trumpet
forceps	plane	sheep	ward
furnace	plough	shovel	wig
glasscutter	prescription	solder	
gun	pulpit	spanner	

Name the main people connected with the following:

army	hospital	police station	school
church	navy	Post Office	ship
college	newspaper	prison	Sunday school
committee	orchestra	railway station	team of players
court of law	Parliament	Salvation Army	workshop

1. What am I called?
    a) I build stone houses.
    b) I carry bags at the railway station.
    c) I write stories for newspapers.
    d) I ride horses in races.
    e) I prepare and sell meat.

2. Many shopkeepers draw attention to their places of business by hanging special signs above their shopdoors. What special sign is displayed by these shopkeepers?
    a) a bootmaker
    b) a chemist
    c) a fishmonger
    d) a hairdresser
    e) a locksmith
    f) an optician
    g) a pawnbroker
    h) a saddler
    i) a watchmaker

3. In each of the following give one word for a person who:
    a) attends to people's teeth
    b) carves in stone
    c) searches for new lands
    d) draws plans for buildings
    e) flies an aeroplane
    f) investigates crime
    g) looks after people's eyes
    h) cares for patients in hospital
    i) repairs boots and shoes
    j) sells from door to door
    k) studies the stars
    l) conducts sales by bidding

4. Arrange the following as you see them advertised in shop windows:
    best assorted, good fresh, fine ripe, splendid cooking, sweet juicy, young spring.
    apples, chocolates, herring, onions, oranges, tomatoes.

Places

Places are usually defined by what they are used for, or where they are located.

Worship

abbey, cathedral, chapel, church, convent, gurdwara, kirk, mandir, monastery, mosque, pagoda, priory, synagogue, tabernacle, temple

Business

What are the places called where the following are made?

beer, bread, films, flour, iron goods, leather, money, paper, ships, whisky

Name particular places where the following are sold:

bread, clothes, fish, flowers, fruit, general foodstuffs, meat, milk, newspapers, poultry, spectacles, sweets and chocolates, tobacco, vegetables, writing materials.

Sport

Give particular names of the places where the following are played:

badminton, bowls, boxing, cricket, croquet, football, golf, hockey, putting, rugby, running, skating, sleighing, tennis, wrestling.

General

Give the particular names of the places connected with the following:

Where	Where
aeroplanes are kept	historical relics are shown
bees are kept	law is meted out
birds are kept	operations are performed
bull-fighting is held	orphans are kept
cars are kept	people are buried
chickens are hatched	people lunch for payment
cooks prepare food	plays are shown
criminals are kept	pupils are educated
doctors receive their patients	rooks build their nests
films are shown	soldiers are stationed
fish are kept	water is stored
fruit trees grow	wild animals are kept
gas is stored	young plants and flowers are reared
grain is stored	young trees are grown
grapes are grown	

Receptacles

It is interesting to note the types of containers used to hold and carry foodstuffs, e.g.

bag – cocoa, coffee, rice, sago, sugar
barrel – apples, beer, oil
box – apples, butter, currants, fish
chest – tea, cloves
sack – flour, potatoes

Exercises on receptacles

1. Name the contents you would expect to find in the following:

barrel	case	jug	sheath
basin	cask	keg	still
basket	cellar	kettle	tank
bath	compact	kitbag	tankard
bin	cup	library	teapot
boiler	cupboard	packet	Thermos (vacuum) flask
bottle	decanter	pan	till
bowl	drum	pitcher	trunk
box	envelope	pocket-book	tub
briefcase	flagon	portfolio	tumbler
butt	flask	pot	urn
caddy	gasometer	punnet	vase
can	goblet	purse	vat
canister	hamper	safe	wallet
carafe	handbag	satchel	wardrobe
carton	jar	scabbard	

2. In what receptacles or containers would you expect to find the following?

Example: tea – caddy.

money _____   jam _____   sword _____

water _____   coal _____   flowers _____

sauce _____   letter _____   wine _____

Sounds and motions

All creatures make sounds and move in a fashion peculiar to their species. Their outstanding characteristics are described by the common adjectives.

Creature	Sound	Motion	Common adjective
ape	gibbers	swings	ungainly
ass	brays	jogs	stupid
bear	growls	lumbers	clumsy
bee	hums	flits	busy
beetle	drones	crawls	horrid
bull	bellows	charges	angry
cat	purrs	steals	sleek
cow	lows	wanders	stolid
deer	bells	bounds	fallow
dog	barks	runs	faithful
donkey	brays	trots	obstinate
elephant	trumpets	ambles	ponderous
frog	croaks	leaps	clammy
horse	neighs	gallops	noble
hound	bays	bounds	gallant
hyena	screams	prowls	cunning
lamb	bleats	frisks	gentle
lion	roars	prowls	tawny
monkey	chatters	climbs	agile
mouse	squeaks	scampers	timid
person	talks	walks	average
pig	grunts	trots	fat
rabbit	squeals	leaps	timid
serpent	hisses	glides	loathsome
wolf	howls	lopes	lean
bird	whistles	flies	swift
cock	crows	struts	proud
crow	caws	flaps	black
curlew	pipes	flits	lonely
duck	quacks	waddles	waddling

Creature	Sound	Motion	Common adjective
eagle	screams	swoops	proud
hen	cackles	struts	domestic
lark	sings	soars	gentle
owl	hoots	flits	tawny
parrot	screeches	flits	saucy
pigeon	coos	flutters	gentle
robin	chirps	hops	little
seagull	screams	glides	tireless
sparrow	chirps	flits	little
swallow	twitters	dives	swift
turkey	gobbles	struts	plump
wren	warbles	hops	tiny

aquiline	– like an eagle	ferine	– like a wild beast
asinine	– like an ass	leonine	– like a lion
bovine	– like a cow or ox	lupine	– like a wolf
canine	– like a dog	ovine	– like a sheep
corvine	– like a crow	piscine	– like a fish
elephantine	– like an elephant	porcine	– like a pig
equine	– like a horse	tigrine	– like a tiger
feline	– like a cat	vulpine	– like a fox

Certain words are used in **imitation** of the sounds made by creatures, e.g.

ass	– hee-haw	**duck**	– quack
cat	– me-ow	**hen**	– cluck
cock	– cock-a-doodle-do	**owl**	– tu-whoo
cow	– moo	**rook**	– caw
cuckoo	– cuckoo	**sheep**	– baa
dog	– woof	**sparrow**	– tweet-tweet

The following verbs are obtained from the **habits** of creatures:

to ape	– to imitate foolishly	to badger	– to worry or tease
to crow	– to boast or swagger	to dog	– to follow or track
to duck	– to dip or plunge	to ferret	– to search out
to fox	– to act cunningly	to hound	– to pursue relentlessly
to ram	– to drive or push into	to wolf	– to eat greedily

Exercises on sounds and motions

1. Animals make different sounds, e.g. The dog **barks**.
   What sounds are made by the following animals?
   donkey, elephant, horse, pig, wolf, monkey, deer, cow, bear, hyena

2. Write the names of the creatures:

   The _____ bays.   The _____ croaks.
   The _____ hisses.   The _____ purrs.
   The _____ crows.   The _____ gobbles.
   The _____ bleats.   The _____ roars.
   The _____ caws.   The _____ quacks.

3. Describe the movements of the following, e.g. The horse **gallops**.

   The frog _____.   The duck _____.
   The monkey _____.   The lamb _____.
   The wolf _____.   The lark _____.
   The seagull _____.   The bear _____.

4. Apply the most fitting adjective:
   sleek, cunning, obstinate, fat, tireless, loathsome, gentle, faithful.

   The _____ mule.   The _____ fox.
   The _____ pig.   The _____ lamb.
   The _____ dog.   The _____ cat.
   The _____ serpent.   The _____ seagull.

5. What is meant by calling a person the following?

   a) an ape   h) a fox   o) a rabbit
   b) an ass   i) a goat   p) a sheep
   c) a bear   j) a horse   q) a snail
   d) a bull   k) a hound   r) a swine
   e) a dog   l) a lamb   s) a tortoise
   f) a donkey   m) a lion   t) a viper
   g) an elephant   n) a pig   u) a wolf

6. Which creatures were the speakers thinking of when they said?
   a) "The man bellowed with rage."
   b) "He has the hump today."
   c) "We were stung by his remarks."
   d) "Don't crow so loudly."
   e) "The officer barked an order."
   f) "The witch spoke in a croaky voice."
   g) "He grunted in reply."
   h) "The children were chattering in the hall."
   i) "Why are you galloping along the corridor?"
   j) "The boy howled when he was caught."
   k) "The wicked old woman cackled loudly as she stirred the pot."
   l) "The lecturer's voice droned on and on."
   m) "The little girl screeched with delight."
   n) "The captain snorted in disgust."
   o) "The curious child prowled about the room."
   p) "Loud hooting interrupted the speech."

7. Explain the words underlined in the following sentences:
   a) He had an <u>aquiline</u> nose.
   b) The burglar walked with a <u>feline</u> tread.
   c) The yokel had a <u>bovine</u> look.
   d) He was scolded for his <u>asinine</u> conduct.
   e) They had the appearance of sharp <u>canine</u> teeth.

8. What feeling is expressed by the following?
   a) a chuckle
   b) a groan
   c) a growl
   d) a grunt
   e) a hoot
   f) a howl
   g) a roar
   h) a screech
   i) a sigh
   j) a sniff
   k) a snort
   l) a squeal

9. Complete the following:
   On a recent visit to a large farm I heard various animal sounds. I heard:
   a cock _____, cows _____, pigs _____, ducks _____,
   horses _____, lambs _____, turkeys _____ and a dog _____.

Sounds made by objects

Note that the words have been formed to resemble the sounds made by the objects.

babble of a stream

bang of a door

beat of a drum

blare of a trumpet

blast of an explosion

booming of a gun

bubbling of water

buzz of a saw

call of a bugle

chime of a bell (large)

chime of a clock

chug of an engine

clang of an anvil

clang of a bell

clanking of chains

clatter of hoofs

clink of a coin

crack of a whip

crackling of wood

creak of a hinge

crinkle of paper

dripping of water

grinding of brakes

gurgle of a stream

hissing of steam

hoot of a horn

howling of the wind

jangling of chains

jingle of coins

lapping of water

lash of a whip

murmur of a stream

patter of feet

patter of rain

pealing of bells

ping of a bullet

popping of corks

purr of an engine

rattling of dishes

report of a rifle

ring of metal

ring of a telephone

ringing of bells

roar of a torrent

rumble of a train

rustle of silk

rustling of leaves

scrape of a bow

screeching of brakes

shriek of a whistle

shuffling of feet

sighing of the wind

singing of the kettle

skirl of the bagpipes

slam of a door

splutter of an engine

swish of skirts

throb of an engine

thunder of hoofs

tick of a clock

tinkle of a bell (small)

tinkle of glass

toot of a horn

tramp of feet

twang of a bow

wail of a siren

whack of a cane

whirring of wings

whoosh of a rocket

Sounds made by objects

Exercises on sounds made by objects

1. Fill in suitable words.
   Example: The **beat** of a drum.
   The _____ of a hinge.　The _____ of a whip.　The _____ of brakes.
   The _____ of steam.　The _____ of feet.　The _____ of silk.
   The _____ of a bugle.　The _____ of a clock.

2. Supply the missing words.
   Example: The clatter of **hoofs**.
   The pealing of _____.　The popping of _____.　The booming of _____.
   The skirl of the _____.　The crinkle of _____.　The throb of an _____.
   The slam of a _____.　The toot of a _____.

3. Use the right words in the following:
   A boiling kettle _____.
   Frying fat _____ in the pan.
   Coins _____ in the bag.
   The heavy bar fell with a _____.
   Suddenly we heard the _____ of hoofs.
   We were awakened by the _____ of the big church clock.
   The passengers heard the loud _____ of brakes.
   The rude boy _____ the door behind him.
   The north wind _____ in the chimney.
   I heard the _____ of a rifle.
   The rain _____ on the window.
   Thunder _____.

4. Complete the following by adding a sentence which indicates the cause of the sound.
   The first is done for you:
   a) Toot! Toot! The sound of a car horn warned us of danger.
   b) Bang! _____.
   c) Boom! _____.
   d) Crash! _____.
   e) Plop! _____.
   f) Rat-tat-tat! _____.
   g) Splash! _____.
   h) Tick-tock! _____.
   i) Ting-a-ling! _____.

Classification

All things on Earth may be divided into two classes:

| Animate (living things) | Inanimate (things having no life) |

1. **The animate or living things** consist of creatures and plants. Creatures can eat, grow and move about from place to place, e.g. animals, including people, birds, fishes, insects, reptiles. Plants are fixed by means of roots and although they can absorb food and grow they cannot move about from place to place, e.g. trees, flowers, vegetables.

2. **The inanimate or things having no life** are fixed, cannot eat, cannot grow and cannot move about from place to place, e.g. stone, cloth, knife.

Every object can be placed in a certain general class either because of its resemblance to other things or because of its purpose or use. **The following are general classes:** animals, birds, insects, fishes, reptiles, flowers, fruits, trees, vegetables, minerals, liquids, apparel, occupations, places, utensils, ships, games, vehicles, cereals, coins, instruments.

Exercises on classification

1. Write one name for each of the following groups, e.g.

    iron, lead, copper: <u>metals</u>

    a) lion, bear, goat, mouse
    b) jacket, blouse, trousers, skirt
    c) canary, eagle, pigeon, magpie
    d) lawyer, butcher, engineer, doctor
    e) beetle, ant, bee, locust
    f) bus, car, lorry, wagon
    g) daffodil, tulip, violet, crocus
    h) cup, saucer, bowl, plate
    i) flounder, haddock, trout, herring
    j) autumn, winter, spring, summer
    k) shoes, sandals, boots, slippers
    l) potato, carrot, beetroot, turnip
    m) hawthorn, palm, beech, chestnut
    n) bread, butter, meat, porridge

o) mango, orange, banana, lemon

p) water, milk, brine, paraffin

q) wheat, maize, oats, barley

r) aunt, uncle, niece, cousin

s) twelve, seven, twenty, eight

t) football, hockey, rugby, cricket

2. In the following lists of words, one word seems out of place. Select the word you consider is not in the same class. The first is done for you.

(1) rose, hibiscus, poinsettia, <u>tomato</u>, carnation

(2) hen, hare, duck, goose, turkey

(3) pine, oak, violet, palm, ash

(4) slate, gold, silver, iron, lead

(5) potato, lemon, maize, cauliflower, spinach

(6) granite, cement, limestone, marble, whinstone

(7) oats, wheat, loaf, sugarcane, barley

(8) salmon, whale, snapper, trout, mullet

(9) diamond, emerald, pearl, ruby, sapphire

(10) Mumbai, London, Washington, Islamabad, Kingston

(11) Ireland, Sri Lanka, Jamaica, Cyprus, Mexico

(12) tea, coffee, cocoa, chocolate, biscuit

(13) rain, sleet, snow, heat, hail

(14) bacon, milk, cheese, butter, bread

(15) shield, lance, dagger, gun, spear

(16) bus, tractor, yacht, train, lorry

(17) cottage, mansion, palace, bungalow, warehouse

(18) tomatoes, journeys, excursions, voyages, trips

(19) birch, maize, maple, chestnut, pine

(20) man, boy, master, princess, uncle

(21) rose, palm, orchid, lily, primrose

(22) Marcus, Maria, Martin, Mohammed, Melvyn

(23) cupboard, kitchen, bathroom, bedroom, hall

(24) orange, potato, cherry, apple, banana

(25) beer, milk, cotton, wine, water

(26) boy, wagon, kitten, girl, puppy

Frangipani

Hibiscus

Zinnia

Coralita

Bougainvillea

(27) plate, cup, saucer, bowl, fork

(28) radiator, saxophone, trumpet, piano, guitar

(29) Pakistan, Spain, Delhi, Brazil, Malaysia

(30) elephant, tiger, giraffe, crocodile, horse

(31) salt, sauce, plate, mustard, pepper

(32) woman, lady, niece, uncle, sister

(33) chair, carpet, wardrobe, stool, table

(34) baker, butcher, fisherman, barber, cook

(35) pigeon, parrot, penguin, sparrow, swallow

(36) basket, purse, kettle, trunk, scabbard

3. Select one of the same kind as the first three in each line. The first is done for you.

(1) cap, balmoral, hat – face, book, <u>turban</u>, coat, hatchet

(2) jug, teapot, cup – bowl, loaf, hammer, key, door

(3) stork, hen, eagle – egg, butterfly, owl, nest, mouse

(4) tulip, daisy, violet – foot, cup, brush, rose, scissors

(5) eye, nose, mouth – hand, leg, knee, arm, ear

(6) tin, copper, zinc – basin, iron, marble, corn, carrot

(7) tuna, swordfish, mackerel – gate, street, orange, ship, trout

(8) chair, table, stool – sofa, pot, door, car, tub

(9) buffalo, monkey, rat – wasp, parrot, lion, canary

(10) apple, banana, plum – peach, violet, onion, hawthorn

(11) iron, lead, copper – marble, coal, slate, zinc

(12) ant, mosquito, moth – rabbit, fly, dog, snake

(13) Nairobi, London, Kingston – Trinidad, Scotland, Kenya, Abuja

(14) steamer, yacht, submarine – aeroplane, trawler, motor, train

(15) caramel, cake, ice-cream – book, pencil, toffee, ruler

(16) flamingo, buzzard, kite – grasshopper, fox, penguin, seal

(17) frock, jacket, coat – blouse, curtain, sheet, carpet

(18) car, train, taxi – bicycle, steamer, canoe, seaplane

(19) tuna, salmon, snapper – vulture, barracuda, snail, cat

(20) tennis, hockey, golf – darts, volleyball, boxing, whist

(21) tulip, geranium, lily – paw-paw, potato, rose, diamond

(22) cocoa, coffee, water – bread, soup, pepper, sugar

(23) violin, piano, harp – drum, bugle, guitar, trombone

(24) cabbage, carrot, potato – lilac, yam, pine, turkey

(25) barber, florist, tailor – miner, driver, cameraman, shoemaker

(26) ankle, foot, knee – head, wrist, thigh, nose

(27) box, vase, bowl – notebook, window, bin, hoe

(28) terrier, collie, greyhound – tiger, spaniel, hyena, lion

(29) sandals, shoes, boots – gloves, trousers, slippers, pockets

(30) oak, pine, fir – teak, lettuce, poinsettia, shark

4. Select the word (in brackets) which has a **similar meaning** to the first three words in each line. The first is done for you.

a) cost, fee, charge   (money, <u>price</u>, purse, silver)

b) mount, soar, rise   (depart, arrive, retire, ascend)

c) hail, greet, salute   (alarm, habit, welcome, ignore)

d) vigilant, alert, wary   (aloft, believe, attempt, watchful)

e) notice, perceive, behold   (provide, observe, advise, obtain)

f) concluded, finished, ended   (commenced, allowed, completed, carried)

g) peace, calm, rest   (quietness, worry, agitated, movement)

h) support, help, aid   (abandon, remedy, assist, ignore)

i) walked, tramped, marched   (chuckled, plodded, glanced, knocked)

j) conquer, defeat, overcome   (bully, retire, vanquish, submit)

k) edge, border, fringe   (margin, centre, interior, cover)

l) occupied, diligent, busy   (lazy, helpless, indolent, industrious)

m) hinder, retard, delay   (progress, obstruct, reveal, select)

n) vagabond, wanderer, tramp   (milliner, caddie, collector, vagrant)

o) desert, forsake, leave   (protect, abandon, pursue, arrive)

p) serious, sober, solemn   (blunt, grave, tired, insulted)

q) weep, cry, wail   (deafen, bite, whimper, frighten)

r) pleased, happy, delighted   (friendly, agreeable, kind, cheerful)

s) stupid, silly, foolish   (stylish, trivial, absurd, helpless)

t) annoy, pester, torment   (deceive, irritate, influence, hinder)

Gradation

Gradation is used to describe relative sizes, ages, colours, etc., a step-by-step scale or series of successive changes. The word comes from the Latin word *gradus*, meaning *step*.

There are five words in each row. You are asked to place them in order of size (smallest first). The first is done for you.

1. boy, baby, man, child, youth

   baby, child, boy, youth, man

2. ten, one, million, thousand, hundred

3. litre, millilitre, decalitre, decilitre, hectolitre

4. year, millennium, century, month, day

5. minute, week, second, hour, day

6. cow, cat, elephant, sheep, mouse

7. kettle, cup, pail, teapot, tub

8. mansion, hut, bungalow, cottage, palace

9. metre, centimetre, kilometre, millimetre

10. shark, sardine, whale, cod, snapper

11. hen, pigeon, robin, ostrich, turkey

12. city, country, town, continent, village

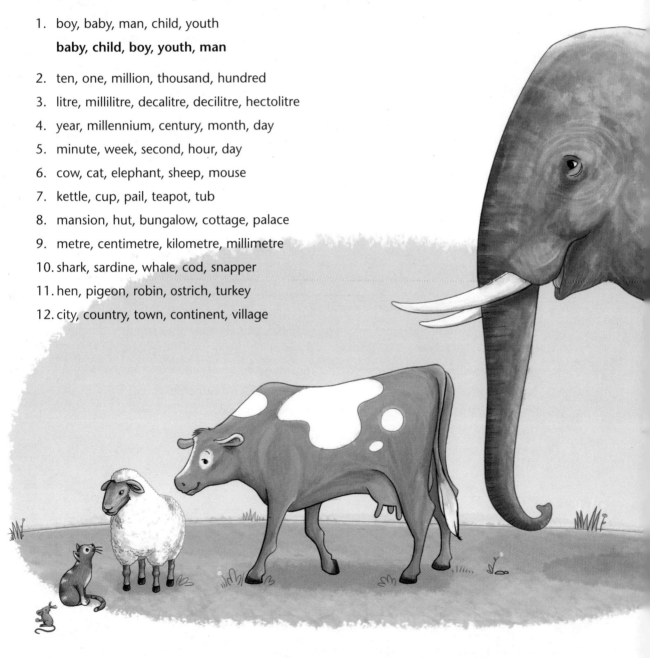

13. bean, pea, cabbage, onion, turnip

14. ocean, river, spring, stream, sea

15. banana, paw-paw, orange, cherry, melon

16. piano, trombone, pipe-organ, violin, flute

17. wallet, purse, safe, vault, handbag

18. fly, midge, ant, wasp, butterfly

19. sentence, letter, paragraph, word, chapter

Here are some harder examples. Grade each group of five words according to the word in bold type (least first):

sound	(giggled, laughed, smiled, guffawed, chuckled)
feeling	(punched, touched, battered, tapped, knocked)
speed	(strode, galloped, trotted, cantered, walked)
sound	(shrieked, talked, shouted, whispered, roared)
feeling	(fingered, slapped, patted, caressed, walloped)
speed	(marched, sauntered, strode, walked, shuffled)
sound	(crooned, hummed, lilted, yodelled, sang)
time	(looked, stared, glimpsed, gazed, glanced)

Association

When there is a link or connection or similarity between different things, they are said to be associated with one another.

Select the two words in the brackets which are associated with (or part of) the first word in bold type. The first is done for you.

1. **boot** (sleeve, <u>heel</u>, handle, <u>sole</u>, paper)
2. **chair** (saucer, poker, arm, tongs, leg)
3. **bed** (mattress, carpet, ribbon, blanket, blouse)
4. **bath** (book, soap, glove, vase, sponge)
5. **room** (flour, ceiling, drum, floor, vegetable)
6. **tree** (wall, trunk, chalk, bough, lamp)
7. **clock** (hands, wristlet, face, shovel, cushion)
8. **flower** (purse, stem, seat, lard, petals)
9. **bird** (sheet, wings, beak, canoe, factory)
10. **bee** (sting, mirror, bread, honey, banana)
11. **knife** (acorn, blade, opposite, handle, coat)
12. **kettle** (spout, plate, butter, basket, lid)
13. **window** (spoon, glass, pillow, bullet, curtains)
14. **car** (chart, anvil, engine, tyres, grate)
15. **sun** (rays, harbour, sermon, heat, crescent)
16. **bottle** (handle, paper, chimney, neck, cork)
17. **rifle** (barrel, trigger, candle, mirror, arrow)
18. **fork** (cellar, prongs, beggar, handle, blade)
19. **fish** (fodder, arms, gills, mutton, fins)
20. **torch** (bulb, furnace, battery, meter, grate)
21. **door** (model, knob, disease, drawer, hinges)
22. **bicycle** (pedals, hangar, bowl, pump, gangway)
23. **pillow** (rug, slip, cloak, bolster, pinafore)
24. **ship** (hood, melody, bridge, trolley, bow)
25. **aeroplane** (funnel, wings, tail, tunnel, paddle)
26. **horse** (bridle, crystal, branch, mane, horns)
27. **fire** (errand, smoke, boots, comb, flame)
28. **piano** (buttons, fatigue, keys, pedals, pencil)
29. **potato** (forest, peelings, bark, gown, chips)
30. **hat** (crown, glue, pouch, brim, pocket)
31. **vehicle** (velvet, brakes, wheels, cotton, scissors)
32. **window** (cords, pane, basin, inventor, easel)

33. **boot**   (knuckle, hatchet, upper, jacket, tongue)
34. **pipe**   (granite, towel, packet, bowl, stem)
35. **tree**   (fork, telegraph, foliage, muslin, cabbage)
36. **fruit**   (marble, core, turnip, rind, salmon)
37. **school**   (horse, teacher, parrot, article, book)
38. **house**   (compartment, gable, cock-pit, scuppers, eaves)
39. **telephone** (paragraph, scabbard, receiver, needle, booth)
40. **barrel**   (fatigue, staves, square, hoops, spokes)

Here are more examples with particular reference to parts of our body and their actions:

ear   (deafness, cantered, listening, noticed, tumbled)
mouth   (pushed, strode, glancing, tasting, chewing)
nose   (smiled, sniffed, walked, odour, roared)
eye   (sang, lashes, laughed, blinked, swinging)
face   (folded, smile, yodelled, grin, toddled)
head   (muttered, sauntered, ache, flying, nodding)
arms   (trotted, mumbled, folded, waving, chanted)
hands   (writing, strolling, kicking, winking, clasping)
legs   (crooned, crossed, fingered, smiling, running)
feet   (dancing, waving, paddling, shouting, grinning)

Analogies

An **analogy** is a comparison between one thing and another. It is usually meant to explain or clarify something.

Select suitable words for the spaces below:

Example: Little is to **big** as **dwarf** is to **giant**.

1. **Spider** is to **fly** as **cat** is to _____.

2. **Sheep** is to **mutton** as **pig** is to _____.

3. **Steamer** is to **pier** as **train** is to _____.

4. **Boy** is to **girl** as _____ is to **woman**.

5. **June** is to **July** as _____ is to **May**.

6. **High** is to **low** as _____ is to **down**.

7. **North** is to _____ as **east** is to **west**.

8. **Uncle** is to _____ as **aunt** is to **niece**.

9. **Soldier** is to _____ as **sailor** is to **navy**.

10. _____ is to **donkey** as **neigh** is to **horse**.

11. _____ is to **hand** as **toe** is to **foot**.

12. _____ are to **birds** as **scales** are to **fish**.

13. **Tear** is to **sorrow** as **smile** is to _____.

14. **Wrist** is to **arm** as **ankle** is to _____.

15. **One** is to **ten** as **ten** is to _____.

16. **Arrow** is to **bow** as _____ is to **rifle**.

17. **Cat** is to **kitten** as _____ is to **pup**.

18. **Foot** is to **man** as _____ is to **horse**.

19. **Father** is to _____ as **mother** is to **daughter**.

20. **Artist** is to _____ as **author** is to **book**.

21. **Water** is to _____ as **liquid** is to **solid**.

22. _____ is to **cygnet** as **pig** is to **piglet**.

23. _____ is to **herring** as **school** is to **whales**.

24. _____ is to **hive** as **cow** is to **cowshed**.

25. **Wing** is to **bird** as **fin** is to _____.

26. **Rich** is to **poor** as **ancient** is to _____.

27. **One** is to **single** as **two** is to _____.

28. **Flock** is to **sheep** as _____ is to **cattle**.

29. **Here** is to **there** as _____ is to **that**.

30. **Day** is to **week** as _____ is to **year**.

31. **Eat** is to _____ as **go** is to **went**.

32. **Oil** is to _____ as **tea** is to **caddy**.

33. **Steam** is to _____ as **smoke** is to **fire**.

34. _____ is to **sty** as **horse** is to **stable**.

35. _____ is to **cold** as **seldom** is to **often**.

36. _____ is to **fish** as **air** is to **bird**.

37. **Table** is to **wood** as **window** is to _____.

38. **Food** is to **hungry** as **drink** is to _____.

39. **Statue** is to **sculptor** as **book** is to _____.

40. **Wheel** is to **spoke** as **flower** is to _____.

41. **Nose** is to **smell** as _____ is to **taste**.

42. **Wrist** is to **cuff** as _____ is to **collar**.

43. **Walk** is to **legs** as _____ is to **wings**.

44. **Island** is to **sea** as _____ is to **land**.

45. **Knife** is to _____ as **gun** is to **shoot**.

46. **Picture** is to _____ as **carpet** is to **floor**.

47. **Graceful** is to _____ as **polite** is to **rude**.

48. **Descend** is to _____ as **ascend** is to **height**.

49. _____ is to **pipes** as **electricity** is to **wires**.

50. _____ is to **church** as **tower** is to **castle**.

51. _____ is to **forest** as **sheep** is to **flock**.

52. _____ is to **egg** as **rind** is to **orange**.

53. **Constable** is to **thief** as **gamekeeper** is to _____.

54. **Whisper** is to **shout** as **walk** is to _____.

55. **Hearing** is to **ear** as **sight** is to _____.

It makes you think

Sometimes you have to think carefully about what you have read, in order to understand the true meaning. Like a detective, you need to be alert for the clues, and make sensible deductions.

1. Here is a list of Christmas presents which arrived at the Browns' house:

   diary, razor, knitting-bag, chocolates, saw, cigarettes, grapes and a fishing-rod.

   a) **Mr Brown** has a beard, likes woodwork, but does not smoke.
   b) **Mrs Brown** is ill in bed, but able to sit up and use her hands.
   c) **John Brown** is twenty years old, clean-shaven, and does not like fishing.
   d) **Mary Brown** is twelve years old, keen on writing, and fond of sweets.

   Distribute the presents on the above list to each member of the family.

2. On one side of my street the homes all have odd numbers, ending with the baker's which is No. 17. On the other side the numbers are all even, ending with the draper's which is No. 18. Fred Thomson is my next-door-neighbour and his house is No. 10. You pass my house when walking from the draper's to Fred's house.

   What number is my house?

3. A policeman was on his rounds one night when he saw a man with a box under his arm come out of a house and hurry down the street. Later the constable found that some jewels had been stolen from the house. The officer remembered that the man he had seen wore a long black coat. He had also noticed that the man had a beard and was lame in his right leg. The next day the following four men were detained:

   John Smith – bearded, long black coat, lame in left leg.

   Tom Taylor – bearded, short black coat, lame in right leg.

   Jack Jones – lame in left leg, short black coat, bearded.

   Jim Baker – long black coat, lame in right leg, bearded.

   If you were the policeman, whom would you consider guilty?

4. The sentences below, when properly arranged, form a short story. Indicate their correct order by numbering them from **1** to **5**:

( ) The lad was cast ashore on a lonely island near the scene of the tragedy.

( ) After many exciting adventures he returned to England none the worse for his experience.

( ) Robinson Crusoe went to sea when he was nineteen years of age.

( ) Luckily he managed to obtain from the wreck many things which proved useful to him during his stay on the island.

( ) On his first voyage, the ship encountered a terrible storm and foundered on a rock.

5. In a very dark cupboard there is a heap of twenty socks, all of the same size, ten of which are grey and ten blue. **How many socks must you pick up** in order to make sure that you obtain **a pair of the same colour?**

6. My clock has gone wrong and chimes three times at one o'clock, four times at two o'clock, and so on. It is also half-an-hour fast. **What is the correct time when the clock has just chimed eight?**

7. Tom is twice as old as Mary, but he is two years younger than Jim. What is Mary's age if Jim will be twenty years old in two years' time?

An odd word or two

Where does a man buy a cap for his knee,
Or a key for a lock of his hair?
Should his eyes be called an academy
Because there are pupils there?

In the crown of his head what gems are found?
Who crosses the bridge of his nose?
Can he use, if a picture requires to be hung,
The nails on the ends of his toes?

If the crook of his elbow is put in gaol,
I'd say, "What did he do?"
But how does he sharpen his shoulder-blades?
I'm hanged if I know. Do you?

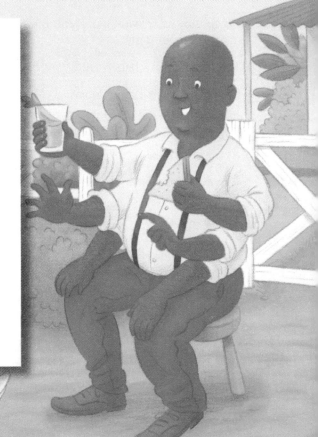

Absurdities

Anything which is absurd is utterly foolish and unreasonable.

Can you explain what is absurd in the following?

1. I had six pencils altogether and gave away three of them to my little brother. I had nine pencils left.

2. To sweeten his tea the boy put a spoonful of salt in it.

3. The man is not so tall as he was when a baby.

4. The express train sped along swiftly and silently as it had square wheels.

5. I hope to attend the concert which took place last week.

6. The witness was asked, "Were you near the horse when it kicked you?"

7. A tramp, wishing to lengthen his blanket, took a bit off the top and added it to the bottom.

8. "Kind sir! Please give me a copper as I am deaf and dumb," cried the old beggar.

9. "Keep moving, please! If everybody was to stand there, how would the rest of the people manage to get past?"

10. The storm, which began yesterday, has continued for three days without a break.

11. "The elephant is a bonnie bird,
    It flits from bough to bough,
    It makes its nest in the rhubarb tree,
    And whistles like a cow."

12. "'Twas in the month of Liverpool,
    In the city of July,
    The rain was snowing heavily,
    And the streets were very dry."

13. Two Inuit were having a chat. The weather was so cold that, when one of them spoke, his words froze into blocks of ice. The other had to melt the blocks in a frying pan in order to find out what his friend had been saying to him.

14. One day at the seaside a man dived from a high platform. When he was half-way down he suddenly noticed that the tide was out and that he would strike his head on the rocks below. This frightened him so much that he changed his mind and jumped back to the platform.

15. A father wrote to his son, "I enclose a postal order. If you do not receive this letter, please let me know at once."

16. A magician was showing his favourite trick. From the roof of the stage hung a long rope, at the end of which was a hook. An assistant entered and placed a pail of water on the hook. Waving his hands and shouting some strange words, the conjurer covered the pail of water with a magic cloth. A few seconds later he snatched the cloth away and, lo and behold! the pail had disappeared and the water was left hanging on the hook.

17. It is much safer to travel in a car than in a train, because in a train accident hundreds of people may be injured, while in a car accident there are never more than a few people injured.

18. The proud owner said to his friend, "This clock is so old that the moving shadow of the pendulum has worn away the wood at the back."

19. In some countries it is against the law for a man to marry his widow's sister.

20. Old John Smith lived in a small cottage, which stood on the top of a barren hill and faced the east. From the foot of the hill a grassy plain stretched in every direction as far as the eye could see. On the evening of John's thirtieth birthday, while he was sitting on the front door-step, watching the setting sun, he noticed a horseman riding down to the cottage. The trees made it difficult for him to see clearly, but he perceived that the horseman had only one arm. When, however, he got a closer view, he recognised the visitor as his son James, who had left home some twenty years before. On seeing his father, James immediately dismounted, ran towards him, and threw his arms round his neck.

Abbreviations

An **abbreviation** is the shortening of a word to fewer letters. These letters are used in place of a word for brevity. It used to be customary to mark abbreviations with a full stop, but now it is quite correct to omit them. In some cases using the stop helps to avoid confusion, e.g. A.1.

@   at

AA   Automobile Association

AD   *Anno Domini* – in the year of our Lord

AIDS   acquired immune deficiency syndrome

a.m.   *ante meridiem* – before noon

A.1   first class (of ships)

BA   Bachelor of Arts

BBC   British Broadcasting Corporation

BC   before Christ

BD   Bachelor of Divinity

BL   Bachelor of Law

BMA   British Medical Association

BSc   Bachelor of Science

C   centigrade or Celsius

CA   chartered accountant

ChB   Bachelor of Surgery

CIA   Central Intelligence Agency

CID   Criminal Investigation Department

CNN   Cable News Network

Co.   Company or County

c.o.d.   cash on delivery

DIY   do-it-yourself

do   ditto

Dr   Doctor

DV   *Deo volente* – God willing

e.g.   *exempli gratia* – for example

ER   Elizabeth Regina – Queen Elizabeth II

Esq.   esquire

etc.   *et cetera* – and the rest

EU   European Union

F   Fahrenheit

ff   following

FIFA   International Football Federation

GCSE   General Certificate of Secondary Education

GDP gross domestic product

GMT Greenwich Mean Time

HE His or Her Excellency

HH His Holiness

HM His or Her Majesty

HMS His or Her Majesty's Ship or Service

hp horse-power

HRH His or Her Royal Highness

IDD International Direct Dialling

i.e. *id est* – that is

IMF International Monetary Fund

inst. instant – this month

IOU I owe you

JP Justice of the Peace

km kilometre

LA Los Angeles

lat. latitude

lbw leg before wicket

LLB Bachelor of Laws

Ltd Limited

MA Master of Arts

MBA Master of Business Administration

MP Member of Parliament

mph miles per hour

Mr Mister

Mrs Mistress

Ms title for a woman (neither Miss nor Mrs)

NASA National Aeronautics and Space Administration

NATO North Atlantic Treaty Organisation

nb *nota bene* – note well, take note

No *numero* – number

NYC New York City

OHMS On His or Her Majesty's Service

OK all correct

OXFAM Oxford Committee for Famine Relief

PAYE pay as you earn

per cent *per centum* – in each hundred

PIA Pakistan International Airlines

PM Prime Minister

p.m. *post meridiem* – after noon

PO Post Office

pp pages

Pres. President

PS *post scriptum* – written after

PTO please turn over

RAC Royal Automobile Club

RAF Royal Air Force

RAM random access memory

RC Roman Catholic

RIP *requiescat in pace* – may he or she rest in peace

RN Royal Navy

ROM read-only memory

RSVP *répondez, s'il vous plaît* – reply, if you please

SA Salvation Army

SS steam-ship or sailing-ship

TA Territorial Army

TUC Trades Union Congress

UK United Kingdom

ult. *ultimo* – last month

UN United Nations

UNESCO United Nations Educational, Scientific and Cultural Organisation

UNICEF United Nations International Children's Emergency Fund

USA United States of America

v *versus* – against

VAT value added tax

viz. *videlicet* – namely

WP word processing / processor

www world wide web

YMCA Young Men's Christian Association

YWCA Young Women's Christian Association

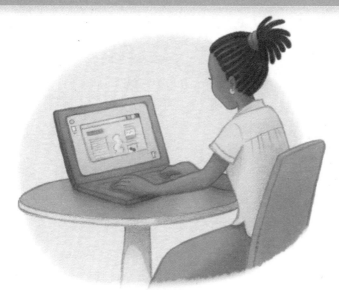

Contractions

auto	automobile
bus	omnibus
cello	violoncello
exam	examination
gym	gymnasium
mag	magazine
phone	telephone
photo	photograph
piano	pianoforte
plane	aeroplane
pram	perambulator
prom	promenade
specs	spectacles

Exercises on abbreviations

1. a) What do the following abbreviations mean?
        BSc, BBC, IDD, MP, PO, BC, MA, HRH, lbw, HMS
    b) Often abbreviations are used in letter-writing. Give the meaning of the following:
        a.m., inst., ult., Esq., Mr, p.m., St

2. Give customary abbreviations for:
    a) Monday, Tuesday, Wednesday, Friday, Saturday, January, February, August,
        September, October, November, December.
    b) ounces, pounds (weight), hundredweights, pints, gallons, seconds, minutes, hours,
        inches, feet, yards, miles.
    c) millimetres, centimetres, metres, kilometres, millilitres, centilitres, litres, milligrams,
        grammes, kilograms, millions.

3. Write the following with all abbreviated terms in full:
    a) Robt. Brown, Esq., 74 Abbey Rd, Glasgow, UK.
    b) Dr Thos. Smith, MP, a brother of the famous Harley St surgeon who recently toured
        the USA, was married on the 4th inst. in St Margaret's Chapel, Westminster.

4. Write the following sentences, using the customary abbreviations:
    a) William Miller of Her Majesty's Ship *Newcastle* was awarded the Victoria Cross for
        gallantry in action.
    b) Mister George Woods, a well-known local Justice of the Peace, was appointed
        managing director of Messieurs Cook and Company, Limited.

5. Where contractions have been used in the following sentences, give the words in full:
    a) We boarded a train as the bus was full.
    b) The specs were discovered in the pram.
    c) I saw his photo in a weekly mag.
    d) He phoned for news of the missing plane.
    e) The exam was held in the gym.

Antonyms

Words which are opposites in meaning are called **antonyms**.

Give the words opposite in meaning to the following:

abroad	chubby	dull	foolish	ignorant
absence	clean	dwarf	foreign	immense
accept	clever	early	found	inferior
adult	coarse	east	free	innocent
alive	cold	easy	freedom	join
ancestor	come	ebb	friend	junior
ancient	conceal	educated	front	juvenile
answer	condemn	empty	frown	land
arrive	confined	enemy	full	last
asleep	confirm	entrance	future	late
assemble	contract	evening	gaunt	lean
back	correct	ever	generous	liberty
backward	coward	everywhere	giant	light
bad	curse	exit	go	live
barren	damp	expand	good	long
beautiful	dark	failure	guilty	lost
bent	day	faint	hard	loud
better	deep	fair	hate	love
big	defeat	fair play	heavy	low
bitter	defend	false	height	mad
black	deny	familiar	hell	maximum
bless	depart	famous	here	merry
bold	depth	fancy	hero	minimum
bottom	die	far	heroic	minority
bow	difficult	fat	hide	miser
bright	dirty	feeble	high	miserable
broad	disperse	fertile	hollow	modern
buy	divide	few	home	morning
captive	down	first	honest	motorist
captivity	drunk	flow	hot	mountain
cheap	dry	foe	humble	moving

multiply	pleasant	sadness	spendthrift	transparent
narrow	plural	safety	stale	truth
native	polite	seldom	stationary	ugly
near	poor	selfish	steep	unite
never	poverty	sell	stern	vacant
new	powerful	senior	straight	vague
night	praise	shallow	strong	valley
noise	present	short	stupid	victory
none	private	show	success	wane
north	prosperity	shut	summer	war
nowhere	proud	singular	superior	wax
numerous	purchase	slovenly	sweet	weak
often	question	slow	take	wealth
old	quiet	small	tall	west
opaque	rapid	smart	tame	wet
open	refuse	smooth	temporary	white
out	retire	sober	there	wild
past	retreat	soft	these	wise
peace	reveal	solid	those	worse
pedestrian	rich	sour	timid	wrong
permanent	right	south	tiny	young
plain	rude	spacious	top	youth

Give the words opposite in meaning to the following:

By adding a prefix

advantage	direct	legible	order	safe
approve	essential	like	patient	sane
audible	fair	lock	perfect	screw
aware	famous	loyal	pleasure	selfish
behave	fire	modest	poisonous	sense
comfortable	happy	moral	polite	tidy
common	human	mortal	possible	transitive
connect	just	necessary	proper	trust
content	kind	noble	pure	twist
convenient	known	normal	regular	visible
correct	legal	obey	reverent	wise

By changing the prefix

ascend, encourage, export, exterior, external, increase, inside

By changing the suffix

careful, cheerful, joyful, merciful, pitiful, useful

The following may be said to be **opposites**:

author	reader		judge	prisoner
detective	criminal		king	subject
doctor	patient		lawyer	client
driver	passenger		leader	follower
employer	employee		parent	child
gamekeeper	poacher		shopkeeper	customer
guardian	ward		speaker	listener
host	guest		teacher	pupil
hunter	quarry			

Exercises on antonyms

1. Write words opposite in meaning to:

   success, visible, praise, transparent, fair play, arrive, nowhere, barren, ancient, wise.

2. Give the opposites (by prefix) of the following:

   audible, behave, known, legible, modest, noble, obedient, regular, sense, pleasant.

3. Provide the opposites of each of the following:

   a) north _____   f) possible _____

   b) entrance _____   g) often _____

   c) rough _____   h) enemy _____

   d) pedestrian _____   i) bitter _____

   e) guilty _____   j) senior _____

4. Give the opposites of the adjectives in the following phrases:

   a) a bright boy   d) a bright colour   g) a bright light

   b) a stormy day   e) a stormy sea   h) a stormy meeting

   c) a wild boy   f) a wild horse   i) a wild flower

5. State the opposites of:

a) an armed man   d) a false gift   g) a soft answer

b) I am sorry   e) a heavy load   h) a mighty army

c) to keep step   f) to sing in tune   i) she was dark

6. Choose the opposites to the underlined word.

   Example: The ball was solid – hollow

   a) It was a beautiful dress.

   b) Tuesday was a very sunny day.

   c) The ascent of the hill took two hours.

   d) He has a temporary post.

   e) She purchased the toy.

   f) He is a lazy fellow.

   g) There was an abundance of fruit.

   h) He gave an intelligent answer.

   i) The sea was rough.

   j) It was very fertile land.

7. Complete the following sentences with a word which is the opposite of the underlined word:

   a) Read the question and then write your _____.

   b) The polar bear which escaped from the zoo was soon _____.

   c) Last year the well was empty but this year it is _____.

   d) A polite boy is much thought of: there is nothing to be gained by being

   _____.

   e) I suddenly remembered that I had _____ my spectacles.

8. Rewrite the following sentences, putting in words opposite in meaning to those underlined:

   a) In the morning the sun rises in the east.

   b) The hero was praised for his fair play.

   c) The fancy box was big and heavy.

   d) Profits on superior articles made him rich.

   e) The mighty army advanced after its success.

Synonyms

Words which are very similar or the same in meaning are called **synonyms**.

abandon	leave		dusk	twilight
abode	dwelling		elude	escape
abundant	plentiful		emperor	king
accused	blamed		enemy	foe
acute	sharp		enormous	gigantic
adhere	stick		extended	enlarged
affectionate	loving		exterior	outside
aid	help		fall	drop
ally	friend		famous	noted
amazement	wonder		fatigue	weariness
ancient	old		feeble	weak
assemble	gather		gap	hole
astonish	surprise		glance	look
asunder	apart		gravely	sternly
blank	empty		greeted	saluted
bright	shining		grope	feel
broad	wide		gruff	harsh
caution	care		halt	stop
circular	round		heroic	brave
coarse	rough		hoax	trick
commence	begin		imitate	copy
comprehend	understand		insolent	rude
conceal	hide		intention	purpose
constable	policeman		interior	inside
conversation	talk		join	unite
courage	bravery		lament	grieve
cunning	sly		lean	thin
curb	control		lofty	high
custom	habit		loyal	true
deceive	cheat		mad	insane
difficult	hard		malady	disease
disaster	calamity		margin	edge

mariner	sailor		remedy	cure
marsh	swamp		residence	dwelling
maximum	most		reveal	show
meagre	scanty		roam	wander
minimum	least		robust	strong
moan	groan		scene	sight
modern	new		shrine	tomb
moisture	dampness		sleek	smooth
mute	dumb		slender	slim
myth	fable		small	little
nimble	agile		squirming	wriggling
noisy	rowdy		steed	horse
odour	smell		stern	strict
omen	sign		stubborn	obstinate
option	choice		sturdy	strong
peculiar	strange		surrender	yield
persuade	coax		suspended	hung
plume	feather		terror	fear
powerful	strong		tested	tried
profit	gain		thrust	pushed
prohibit	forbid		tranquil	peaceful
prompt	quick		transparent	clear
protect	guard		unite	join
puny	weak		vacant	empty
purchase	buy		valour	bravery
quaint	odd		vanquish	defeat
quantity	amount		wealth	riches
queer	peculiar		wicked	sinful
raiment	clothes		withdraw	retire
ramble	roam		wrath	anger
rank	position		wretched	miserable
rapid	quick		yearly	annually
regret	sorrow			

Exercises on synonyms

1. Give words similar in meaning to the following:

   comprehend, empty, sufficient, vicinity, attempted, enemies, risky, purchase, perceive, modern.

2. In the spaces provided write words similar in meaning:
   a) bright _____
   b) convenient _____
   c) disappear _____
   d) hoax _____
   e) valour _____
   f) peculiar _____
   g) lofty _____
   h) unite _____
   i) margin _____
   j) wrath _____

3. Place the words in their proper positions in the sentence:

   (handsome – pretty)   The _____ girl admired the _____ portrait.

   (proud – vain)   The _____ king laughed at the _____ little girl.

   (fat – stout)   A _____ person should not eat _____ meat.

   (feeble – weak)   _____ tea will not refresh the _____ old lady.

   (hot – sultry)   On a _____ day don't drink _____ liquids.

   (old – antique)   The _____ man was fond of _____ furniture.

   (loving – tender)   Her _____ hands had prepared a _____ chicken.

   (sad – dull)   The day was _____ and we felt quite _____.

4. Give short sentences, one for each word, showing the correct use of the following:

   learn, teach   invent, discover

   possible, probable   accept, except.

5. Use similar words in place of the underlined words:
   a) The bucket dropped into the well.
   b) Don't conceal your real feelings.
   c) I was astonished to find the house vacant.
   d) He alters his plans annually.

Homonyms and homophones

A **homonym** is a word having the same sound, and perhaps the same spelling, as another, but with a different meaning. **Homophones** sound the same but are spelt differently from each other. They also have different meanings. The words below are all homophones.

air	heir	feat	feet
aisle	isle, I'll	flew	flue
allowed	aloud	flour	flower
ate	eight	foul	fowl
bail	bale	gait	gate
ball	bawl	gamble	gambol
bare	bear	gilt	guilt
beach	beech	grate	great
bell	belle	groan	grown
blew	blue	hail	hale
boar	bore	hair	hare
board	bored	hear	here
bough	bow	heard	herd
boy	buoy	higher	hire
buy	by, bye	him	hymn
ceiling	sealing	hoard	horde
cellar	seller	hole	whole
cereal	serial	holy	wholly
cheap	cheep	hour	our
check	cheque	key	quay
coarse	course	knew	new
core	corps	knight	night
council	counsel	knot	not
crews	cruise	knows	nose
currant	current	leak	leek
dear	deer	lightening	lightning
die	dye	loan	lone
draft	draught	loot	lute
ewe	you, yew	made	maid
faint	feint	mail	male
fair	fare	main	mane

mare	mayor	sail	sale
meat	meet	scene	seen
medal	meddle	scent	sent, cent
missed	mist	sea	see
muscle	mussel	seam	seem
oar	ore	sew	so, sow
pail	pale	sight	site
pain	pane	soar	sore
pair	pare, pear	sole	soul
pause	paws	son	sun
peace	piece	stair	stare
peal	peel	stake	steak
peer	pier	stationary	stationery
place	plaice	steal	steel
plain	plane	stile	style
plum	plumb	tail	tale
pores	pours	tears	tiers
practice	practise	their	there
praise	prays, preys	threw	through
principal	principle	throne	thrown
profit	prophet	tide	tied
rains	reigns, reins	time	thyme
raise	rays, raze	to	too, two
read	reed	told	tolled
real	reel	vain	vane, vein
right, rite	wright, write	vale	veil
ring	wring	waist	waste
road	rode, rowed	wait	weight
root	route	weak	week
rose	rows	wood	would
rye	wry		

Exercises on homonyms and homophones

1. Make short sentences, one for each word, showing the correct use of the following:
   bear, bare, flower, flour, too, two, ate, eight, write, right.

2. Cross out the wrong words:
   She bought some (steak, stake).
   The bicycle was for (sail, sale).
   We must (hire, higher) a car.
   The (hole, whole) army marched into the town.
   The boy broke a (pane, pain) of glass.
   We walked to the golf (coarse, course).
   (Their, There) books are on the desks.
   The girl had to (wait, weight) till four o'clock.
   The wounded soldier uttered a loud (grown, groan).
   The joiner (bored, board) a small (whole, hole) in the (wood, would).

3. Give sentences, one for each word, showing clearly the meaning of each of the following words:
   pause, paws, steal, steel, heard, herd, reign, rain, their, there.

4. Insert the words in their proper places:
   (allowed – aloud)   We are not _____ to speak _____ in class.
   (maid – made)   The _____ admitted that she had _____ a mistake.
   (piece – peace)   He will give us no _____ until he receives a _____ of cake.
   (scent – sent)   "Did you get the _____ I _____ you?" he asked.
   (stair– stare)   I saw him _____ at the man on the _____.
   (waist – waste)   "_____ not, want not," said the woman with the thin _____.

5. Medal, horde, gambol, guilt, prophet, gamble, meddle, profit, gilt, hoard.
   From the above list insert the correct words in the following sentences:
   A _____ of coins was found under the floor.
   The business man made a large _____ on the deal.
   He was told not to _____ with the toys.
   I saw the lambs _____ in the field.
   His name was printed in large _____ letters.

6. The answers are words that are pronounced alike but differ in meaning, e.g.
    nay (meaning "no") and **neigh** (the cry of a horse).

a)   { a female sheep
     { an evergreen tree

b)   { sandy shore
     { kind of tree

c)   { guided
     { a metal

d)   { opens lock
     { harbour

e)   { flat land
     { joiner's tool

f)   { suffering
     { piece of glass

g)   { something round
     { shout loudly

h)   { rough
     { place for golf

i)   { front of ship
     { branch of tree

j)   { gain
     { foretells future

k)   { a flight of steps
     { to look fixedly

l)   { sixty minutes
     { belonging to us

m)   { quietness
     { a part of anything

n)   { a stupid person
     { no empty space

o)   { in that place
     { belonging to them

Verbs

Verbs are **doing** words we say, giving **doing** a very broad meaning. Words for **being done**, even **existing** (doing nothing) are verbs. Sometimes a verb consists of **one** word, sometimes of **two** or **more**. Here are some examples.

a) Dogs *bark*.

b) Tom *laughed*.

c) *Is* Mary there?

d) *Go* away!

e) The day *will come*.

f) The jet *is landing*.

g) No words *were spoken*.

h) Guests *will be invited*.

i) The tiger *should have waited*.

j) My house *was being repaired*.

k) You *must have been joking*.

Note: One of the words in the verb is the **main** verb: the others are **auxiliaries** (helpers).

Identify the verbs in the following sentences:

1. Rain fell yesterday.
2. Day is dawning.
3. It is sunny today.
4. We have been robbed.
5. I do not smoke.
6. I could hardly see.
7. Uncle may be coming today.
8. We should have been patient.
9. You should not have been told.
10. They are not looking well.
11. The sheep were worried by dogs.
12. I was worried till you came.

Forms and parts of verbs

Different forms have different uses, for example:

singular and plural subjects	A dog *barks*; dogs *bark*
different pronoun subjects	I *think*; he *thinks*
present, past, future tense (time)	I *walk*; I *walked*; I *shall walk*
continuous, completed action	We *are looking*; we *have looked*

Infinitive	The **infinitive** (e.g. *to bark, to look*) is the basic form from which most other parts of most verbs can be formed.

The **present** and **past participles** are partly verb and partly adjective.

Present participle	The **present participle** is formed by adding *-ing* to the infinitive and is used with parts of the verb *to be* to form continuous tenses, as in *We are looking* (look + ing).

Past participle	The **past participle** is usually formed by adding *-ed* to the infinitive and is used with parts of the verb *to have* to form perfect (completed action) tenses, as in *We have looked* (look + ed). **Irregular** verbs form their past participle in other ways. Examples are listed on the next page.

Some participles also serve purely as adjectives, e.g. A *dazzling* light; your story was *amusing*; my heart is *broken*; *cracked* cups.

Tenses

Except in the case of the verb *to be*, the **present tense** has the same form as the infinitive (unless the subject is *he, she, it* or a noun, when *-s* or *-es* is added). To form the **future tense** we place *shall* or *will* in front of the infinitive. To form the **past tense** of **regular** verbs we add *-ed* to the infinitive. So we have:

Infinitive	Present tense	Future tense	Past tense
(to) look	(I, they) look (he, it) looks	(I, we) shall look (you, etc.) will look	(I, etc.) looked

So, in **regular** verbs the same form serves both the **past tense**, (I) *looked*, and the **past participle** (I have) *looked*. Many **irregular** verbs, however, form them differently. Here are a few of them:

Present tense	Past tense	Past participle	Present tense	Past tense	Past participle
am	was	been	choose	chose	chosen
arise	arose	arisen	come	came	come
drive	drove	driven	do	did	done
awake	awoke	awakened	drink	drank	drunk
bear	bore	borne	eat	ate	eaten
beat	beat	beaten	fall	fell	fallen
begin	began	begun	fly	flew	flown
ring	rang	rung	forget	forgot	forgotten
sing	sang	sung	freeze	froze	frozen
swim	swam	swum	give	gave	given
bite	bit	bitten	go	went	gone
hide	hid	hidden	lie	lay	lain
blow	blew	blown	ride	rode	ridden
grow	grew	grown	write	wrote	written
know	knew	known	run	ran	run
draw	drew	drawn	shake	shook	shaken
break	broke	broken	tear	tore	torn
speak	spoke	spoken			

Errors

One of the worst errors in speech (and writing) is the use of the past participle instead of the past tense (e.g. I *seen* you; they *done* that), and the past tense instead of the past participle (e.g. Have you *broke* it; they have *went*). To tune your ear to the correct usage give each of the above past tenses a subject (e.g. *Tom drove*) and say it aloud; then put a subject with *have, has* or *had* in front of the past participle (e.g. *I had* driven) and say it aloud.

Exercises on verbs

1. Give the past tense of:
   arise, break, cut, fall, keep, say, shake, drink, bite, choose.

2. Give the past participle of:
   bear, drive, fly, give, hurt, ride, sell, speak, come, swim.

3. Give the present tense of:
   ate, beaten, froze, hidden, blew, spoken, awoke, sold, lost.

4. a) Give the present participle of:
      throw, give, spring, fire, begin.

   b) Give the present infinitive of:
      burn, speak, stand, sweep, drive.

5. Give the past tense and past participle of:
   am, do, forget, grow, write, sing, tear, hide, go, begin.

6. Complete the following table:

Present tense	Past tense	Past participle
I rise	I rose	I have risen
I forget	I _____	I have _____
I cut	_____	_____
I sing	_____	_____
I blow	_____	_____

7. Fill in each space correctly with one of these words:
   rise, rose, raise, risen, raised.
   a) He _____ his hand to greet his friend.
   b) Yesterday the boy _____ at five o'clock.
   c) I saw him _____ from his seat.
   d) She tried to _____ the lid.
   e) The sun had _____ in the sky.

8. Use the correct part of the verbs in the blank spaces:

(go)   She had ＿＿＿＿＿＿＿ for a walk.

(see)   He ＿＿＿＿＿＿＿ his uncle yesterday.

(fall)   The old man ＿＿＿＿＿＿＿ asleep in his chair.

(awake)   He was ＿＿＿＿＿＿＿ by the noise.

(dream)   The boy was ＿＿＿＿＿＿＿ about pirates.

In each of the sentences below there are groups of two words within brackets. One of the two words is correct, the other wrong. Underline the correct word.

1. We (drank, drunk) our tea before we (sung, sang) the carol.

2. After he had (ran, run) about 5 kilometres, he (sank, sunk) to the ground.

3. Some cloth is (wove, woven) from wool which has (grown, grew) on sheep.

4. He had (gave, given) me the parcel before he was (took, taken) a prisoner.

5. The timid creature was (drove, driven) into a narrow valley where it was (slew, slain) by the cruel tiger.

6. The vessel (sank, sunk) before they had (swam, swum) a great distance.

7. The tree had (fell, fallen) across the road and many of its branches were (broke, broken).

8. By the time the sun had (rose, risen) the aeroplane had (flown, flew) across the sea.

9. No sooner had he (spoke, spoken) than a deer (sprang, sprung) into our path.

10. He (began, begun) to look for the toy which he had (gave, given) to his brother.

11. The man had (threw, thrown) away the purse which was (stole, stolen) from the lady.

12. The jacket had been well (wore, worn) and the cloth had (shrank, shrunk).

13. After we had (ate, eaten) our supper we went to the pond which was (froze, frozen) over.

14. The picture was (drawn, drew) by a famous and wealthy artist who had (rose, risen) from poverty.

15. They had just (went, gone) when we were (saw, seen) by our friends.

16. A nest had (fell, fallen) to the ground, where it had been (blew, blown) by the wind.

17. The bell (rang, rung) just after I had (wrote, written) the letter.

Adjectives

An **adjective** is a word which qualifies or adds to the meaning of a noun. (An old form for **adjective** was **ad-noun**.)

Adjectives may be divided into three main classes.

Descriptive adjectives

good, bad, hard, soft, old, young, pale, red

Example: The **old** man caught a **bad** cold.

Adjective of quantity

a) **Definite** (including numerals)
   one, seven, twenty, second, fifth, both, double
   Example: Both players scored **three** goals in the **second** game.

b) **Indefinite**
   all, any, few, many, much, several, some
   Example: We met **several** boys who had caught **some** fish.

Adjectives of distinction

a) **Demonstrative**
   this, that, these, those, yon, yonder
   Example: This stone was found on **yonder** hill.

b) **Interrogative**
   which, what, whose
   Example: Which book do you want?

c) **Distributive**
   each, every, either, neither
   Example: He could go home by **either** route.

Underline the **adjectives** in the following sentences:

1. The tall gentleman wore a blue overcoat.
2. Little Jim was a delicate boy with pale cheeks.
3. The weather was wet and foggy.
4. The ugly old witch spoke in a hoarse cracked voice.
5. The lost ball was found near the wooden gate.

Comparison of adjectives

Adjectives can have three *degrees*: **positive**, **comparative**, **superlative**.

The **positive** is simply descriptive, describing a noun or pronoun, e.g. a *short* holiday; *beautiful* hats; *clever* pupils; this is *broken*.

The **comparative** is used in comparing some creature, thing or group with **one** other (creature, thing or group). e.g. the *taller* of the two; *taller* than the rest; mice are *smaller* than rats. If the positive is a short word, then the comparative is usually formed by adding *-er* to the positive, e.g. fast-er; great-er.

The **superlative** is used in comparing some creature, thing or group with **more than one** other, e.g. the *tallest* of the three; the *wisest* of men. It is usually formed by adding *-est* to the positive, if a short word. When one thing or creature is compared with more than one other **treated as a group**, the comparative is used, e.g. Tom is *taller* than *the rest of the class*.

Adjectives of three syllables or more, and most adjectives of two syllables, form their comparative by placing *more* in front of the positive, and the superlative by placing *most* in front.

Some adjectives have quite different words for the comparative and superlative.

a) Small word in positive:

Positive	Comparative	Superlative	Positive	Comparative	Superlative
big	bigger	biggest	late	later	latest
fast	faster	fastest	long	longer	longest
happy	happier	happiest	small	smaller	smallest
great	greater	greatest	tall	taller	tallest
clever	cleverer	cleverest	narrow	narrower	narrowest

b) Different word for comparative and superlative:

Positive	Comparative	Superlative	Positive	Comparative	Superlative
bad	worse	worst	little	less	least
far	farther	farthest	many	more	most
good	better	best	much	more	most

c) Longer word in positive:

Positive	Comparative	Superlative
beautiful	more beautiful	most beautiful
careful	more careful	most careful
comfortable	more comfortable	most comfortable
ignorant	more ignorant	most ignorant

Exercises on comparison of adjectives

1. Give the comparatives and superlatives of:
   many, hot, bad, famous, little.

2. Write the comparatives of:
   fast, good, gracious, tall, beautiful.

3. Write the superlatives of:
   thin, much, comfortable, handsome.

4. Complete the following table:

Positive	Comparative	Superlative
long	longer	longest
far	_____	_____
good	_____	_____
generous	_____	_____
late	_____	_____
cautious	_____	_____

5. State whether the following words are positive, comparative or superlative:

   nearest, better, far, more certain, surest, larger, most wonderful, bad, shorter, biggest.

6. Correct the following sentences:
   a) James was the biggest of the twins.
   b) A more kinder lady you could not meet.
   c) The best team won the football match.
   d) Fred was the most fast of all the runners.
   e) Who is the tallest, Jack or Betty?
   f) He proved to be the ignorantest person.
   g) Of the two, I like George best.
   h) A badder boy I have never known.
   i) The sailor lifted the thinnest end of the rope.
   j) The patient made the wonderfulest recovery.

Adverbs

An **adverb** is a word which modifies or adds to the meaning of a verb, an adjective, or another adverb.

Adverbs may be divided, according to their use, into the following classes:

a) **Time** – before, now, since, then, already, soon, seldom.
   Example: We have met **before**.

b) **Place** – here, there, everywhere, nowhere.
   Example: They came **here** yesterday.

c) **Manner** – badly, easily, slowly, well.
   Example: The tall boy won **easily**.

d) **Degree** – almost, much, only, quite, very, rather.
   Example: The old lady walked **very** slowly.

e) **Number** – once, twice.
   Example: They ran **twice** round the park.

f) **Questioning** – where, when, how.
   Example: **When** did you see him?

g) **Affirmation** and **negation** – yes, certainly, no, not.
   Example: She can **certainly** swim. I have **not** read the book.

(Many adverbs are often used as connecting words and therefore become conjunctions. You will read about them on page 108.)

The majority of adverbs are formed from corresponding adjectives by adding -*ly*, e.g. quickly, bravely, seriously, happily, clearly, slowly, quietly, angrily, fatally, suitably.

Exercises on adverbs

Underline the **adverbs** in the following sentences:

1. Dinner will soon be ready.
2. There lay the object of our search.
3. The man walked slowly across the field.
4. The apples were quite good.
5. I once saw an eagle kill a rabbit.
6. Where did you find that knife?
7. He can certainly boast about his adventures.
8. The story ended happily.

Comparison of adverbs

Adverbs are compared in the same way as **adjectives**. As most adverbs are two-syllable words or longer they generally form the comparative and superlative by adding **more** and **most** to the positive.

	Positive	Comparative	Superlative
Regular (i)	early	earlier	earliest
	fast	faster	fastest
	long	longer	longest
	soon	sooner	soonest
Regular (ii)	bitterly	more bitterly	most bitterly
	bravely	more bravely	most bravely
	briefly	more briefly	most briefly
	carefully	more carefully	most carefully
	clearly	more clearly	most clearly
	cruelly	more cruelly	most cruelly
	easily	more easily	most easily
	freely	more freely	most freely
	greedily	more greedily	most greedily
	happily	more happily	most happily
	loudly	more loudly	most loudly
	quickly	more quickly	most quickly
	slowly	more slowly	most slowly
	willingly	more willingly	most willingly
Irregular	badly	worse	worst
	far	farther	farthest
	forth	further	furthest
	ill	worse	worst
	late	later	last
	much	more	most
	well	better	best

Some common verbs with suitable adverbs

Verbs	Adverbs
acted	quickly, suddenly, warily
answered	correctly, immediately, angrily
ate	greedily, hungrily, quickly, slowly
bled	freely, profusely, slightly
bowed	humbly, respectfully, stiffly
caressed	fondly, gently, lovingly
charged	bravely, desperately, furiously
chuckled	artfully, gleefully, happily
crept	quietly, silently, softly, stealthily
decided	carefully, eventually, immediately
explained	briefly, clearly, concisely
fell	heavily, quickly, suddenly
flogged	brutally, cruelly, unmercifully
fought	bravely, furiously, gamely
frowned	angrily, sulkily
injured	accidentally, fatally, seriously, slightly
left	hurriedly, quietly, suddenly
listened	anxiously, attentively, carefully
lost	badly, heavily, sportingly
mumbled	angrily, inaudibly, indistinctly
pondered	deeply, seriously, thoughtfully
pulled	hastily, strongly, vigorously

Verbs	Adverbs
ran	hurriedly, quickly, rapidly, slowly
remembered	clearly, distinctly, faintly, slightly
sang	loudly, softly, sweetly, tunefully
shone	brightly, brilliantly, clearly, dimly
shouted	frantically, joyfully, jubilantly, loudly, suddenly
slept	fitfully, lightly, soundly
smiled	broadly, happily, ruefully
sneered	insolently, impudently, tauntingly
spent	foolishly, freely, recklessly, sparingly
spoke	clearly, distinctly, earnestly, loudly, plainly, slowly
sprang	hurriedly, lightly, quickly, suddenly
staggered	awkwardly, drunkenly, weakly
strove	bravely, desperately, manfully
stuttered	excitedly, haltingly, painfully
trembled	fearfully, frightfully, visibly
waited	patiently, anxiously
walked	clumsily, haltingly, quickly, slowly, smartly
wept	bitterly, distractedly, sadly, touchingly
whispered	audibly, quietly, softly
yielded	stubbornly, weakly, willingly

Exercises on adverbs

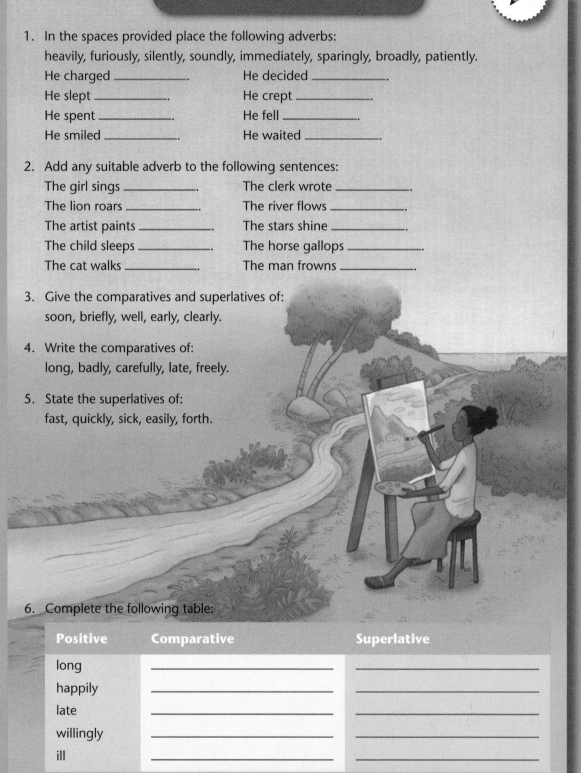

1. In the spaces provided place the following adverbs:
   heavily, furiously, silently, soundly, immediately, sparingly, broadly, patiently.

   He charged _____.   He decided _____.

   He slept _____.   He crept _____.

   He spent _____.   He fell _____.

   He smiled _____.   He waited _____.

2. Add any suitable adverb to the following sentences:

   The girl sings _____.   The clerk wrote _____.

   The lion roars _____.   The river flows _____.

   The artist paints _____.   The stars shine _____.

   The child sleeps _____.   The horse gallops _____.

   The cat walks _____.   The man frowns _____.

3. Give the comparatives and superlatives of:
   soon, briefly, well, early, clearly.

4. Write the comparatives of:
   long, badly, carefully, late, freely.

5. State the superlatives of:
   fast, quickly, sick, easily, forth.

6. Complete the following table:

Positive	Comparative	Superlative
long	_____	_____
happily	_____	_____
late	_____	_____
willingly	_____	_____
ill	_____	_____

Word building

Practise your word building below.

Form nouns from:

able	bright	enter	judge	punctual
absent	cash	equal	just	punish
abundant	child	exceed	know	pursue
accurate	choose	exhaust	laugh	ready
acquaint	civilise	expect	lazy	real
act	clean	explain	learn	rebel
admire	collect	faithful	like	receive
adopt	commence	false	listen	recognise
advertise	compare	famous	live	relieve
allow	conclude	favourite	long	remember
amuse	confident	feed	lose	renew
angry	confuse	fierce	loyal	repeat
anxious	content	fly	magic	repent
appear	create	fragrant	manly	resent
applaud	credit	free	marry	reveal
apply	cruel	friend	merry	revive
approve	curious	grand	mission	sad
arrive	dark	great	mock	satisfy
ascend	deceive	grow	moral	scene
assist	decent	happy	mountain	school
attend	decide	hate	move	scientific
attract	deep	hero	music	secure
bag	defend	high	occupy	see
beautiful	depart	holy	oppose	select
beg	describe	imagine	persuade	serene
begin	destroy	imitate	please	serve
behave	develop	inform	proclaim	shade
believe	discover	injure	profess	sick
bitter	divide	interfere	prosper	simple
boy	do	introduce	proud	speak
brave	encourage	invent	prove	steal
breathe	enjoy	invite	provide	stream

strike	tell	vain	warm	wide
strong	think	various	weak	wise
succeed	thrive	visit	weary	worthy
superior	typical	war	weigh	young

Form adjectives from:

ability	colony	father	Italy	notice
accident	comfort	fault	joy	oak
admire	conclude	favour	law	obey
adventure	continent	fire	learn	occasion
affection	courage	five	length	oppose
angel	coward	fool	life	ornament
anger	craft	force	love	parent
anxiety	credit	forget	luxury	patience
athlete	crime	fortune	man	peace
attract	critic	France	marvel	peril
autumn	cruelty	friend	meddle	person
beauty	custom	giant	melody	picture
Bible	danger	girl	mercy	pity
boy	deceive	gold	metal	please
brass	decide	grace	mine	poet
breath	describe	grief	mischief	poison
Britain	destroy	harm	mock	pride
care	disaster	hate	mountain	prosper
caution	distance	heat	mourn	quarrel
centre	duty	height	move	rag
change	energy	hero	music	reason
charity	enjoy	hope	mystery	science
child	exceed	imagine	nation	sense
choir	expression	industry	nature	shadow
choose	faith	inform	neglect	shower
circle	fame	introduce	noise	silk
collect	fashion	iron	north	silver

sister	strength	tide	victory	winter
skill	study	tire	voice	wisdom
sorrow	success	trouble	volcano	wit
south	sun	truth	Wales	wood
spire	sympathy	type	war	wool
spirit	talk	union	water	worth
star	terror	value	wave	wretch
stop	thirst	vanity	weary	year
storm	thought	variety	west	youth

Form verbs from:

able	courage	frost	long	shelf
actor	creator	full	magnet	short
banishment	critic	glass	moisture	simple
bath	custom	glory	nation	soft
beauty	dark	gold	obedience	solution
blood	deed	grass	peril	song
bright	description	grief	pleasure	spark
broad	dictation	growth	proof	speech
camp	education	horror	provision	strong
circle	false	imitation	pure	success
circulation	fat	joy	relief	terror
civil	fertile	just	resident	thought
clean	fine	knee	resolution	tight
cloth	food	knowledge	rich	tomb
colony	force	large	roll	trial
composition	friend	life	sharp	wide

Form adverbs from:

ability	happy	joy	sweet	true
critic	heavy	pure	terror	weary
faith	horror	simple	thought	wide

Compound words

A word in its simplest form is called a **primary word**, e.g. table, board, egg. If we combine two primary words to form one word we get a **compound word**, e.g. tablecloth, blackboard, eggcup.

Form compound words from the following:

ache	cup	guard	maid	pot	strong
ball	day	gun	man	room	table
black	door	hat	master	safe	tea
board	dust	heart	mat	school	time
boot	egg	house	milk	servant	tomb
cart	fall	jam	mill	shed	tooth
church	fire	lace	out	shop	thrift
cloth	fly	lamp	pick	son	water
coal	foot	life	piece	spend	wife
craft	gentle	light	pond	stand	witch
cry	grand	load	post	stone	yard

Exercises on word building

1. Make a noun corresponding to each of the following words:
   a) please _____
   b) prove _____
   c) know _____
   d) proud _____
   e) choose _____
   f) encourage _____
   g) strong _____
   h) real _____
   i) just _____
   j) give _____

2. Give nouns formed from:
   select, grow, bag, act, receive, invite, succeed, repent, divide.

3. By adding a suffix, form a noun from each of the following:
   astonish, coward, critic, trick, assist, free, inform, loyal, invent, sick.

4. Make an adjective corresponding to each of the following words:
   Britain, heat, expense, anger, faith, height, fashion, boy, vanity, sense.

5. Give adjectives from:
   a) decide _____
   b) Bible _____
   c) talk _____
   d) circle _____
   e) attract _____
   f) mystery _____
   g) voice _____
   h) nation _____
   i) winter _____
   j) peril _____

6. Give a verb corresponding to each of the following words:
   Example: solution – **solve**
   a) knee _____
   b) strong _____
   c) description _____
   d) gold _____
   e) custom _____
   f) tight _____
   g) grief _____
   h) large _____
   i) glory _____
   j) food _____

7. Give verbs from:
   obedient, sweet, education, fat, life, composition, civil, tomb, bath, pure.

8. Form adverbs from:
   anger, tune, excitement, freedom, anxiety, frantic, worry, serious, fool, silence.

9. Complete the following compound words:

_____board   milk_____   grand_____

hat_____   _____cup   _____post

lamp_____   _____cloth   _____ball

tooth_____   book_____   _____stool

10. Complete the following table:

Adjective	Noun	Verb
long	length	lengthen
strong	_____	_____
broad	_____	_____
glad	_____	_____
able	_____	_____
wide	_____	_____

11. Make sentences, two for each word, using the following words
    a) as nouns, and
    b) as adjectives:
    brick, chief, diamond, garden, iron, light, music, sole, square, summer, young.

12. Write sentences, two for each word, using each of the following words first as a noun and then as a verb:
    brush, cycle, fire, heat, hope, notice, sail, saw, spring, step, turn, wave.

13. What part of speech is the word **round** in each of the following sentences?
    a) It was a large **round** table.
    b) The tourist played a **round** of golf.
    c) The speaker turned **round**.
    d) The boy ran quickly **round** the field.
    e) The horses must **round** this corner.

Concord

Concord means agreement or harmony. In grammar we apply this word as meaning perfect agreement between subject and verb. This is shown by the subject and verb having the same person and number.

1. When the **subject** is **singular**, the **verb** is **singular**, e.g.
   a) He writes.
   b) She swims.
   c) The baby cries.

2. When the **subject** is **plural**, the **verb** is **plural**, e.g.
   a) We write.
   b) They swim.
   c) The babies cry.

3. Expressions such as **each of**, **one of**, **neither of**, **every one of**, **not one of** and words such as **each**, **every**, **none**, **anybody**, **everybody** and **nobody** must be followed by **verbs** in the **singular**, e.g.
   a) **Each of** the boys **has** a toy.
   b) **One of** the ladies **is** married.
   c) **Neither of** the brothers **was** present.
   d) **Is either of** the sisters coming?
   e) **Every one of** us **knows** that it is wrong.
   f) **Not one of** the girls **has** a skipping rope.
   g) **Each** man **was** searched.
   h) **Every** child **has** a secret ambition.
   i) **Anybody is** admitted to the caves.
   j) **Everybody was** delighted at the close.
   k) **Nobody is** displeased with the result.
   l) **None** of the ships **was** lost.

4. A **singular subject** with attached phrases introduced by **with** or **like** or **as well as** is followed by a **singular verb**, e.g.
   a) The boy, **with** several others, **was** late for school.
   b) Alice, **like** Rose, **is** tall for her age.
   c) Tom, **as well as** Fred, **rises** early in the morning.

5. When a **verb** has **two singular subjects** connected by **and** the verb is **plural**, e.g.
   a) The cat **and** the dog **were** great friends.
   b) The farmer **and** his wife **are** jolly people.

6. When a **verb** has **one or more plural subjects** connected by **and**, the **verb** is **plural**, e.g.
   a) The officer **and** his men **were** crossing the field.
   b) The boys **and** the girls **are** sure of their work.

7. **Two singular subjects** separated by "either _____ or", "neither _____ nor" take a **singular verb**, e.g.

   a) **Either** one **or** the other **has** blundered.

   b) **Either** he **or** she **is** right.

   c) **Neither** Grace **nor** Helen **knows** anything about it.

   d) **Neither** he **nor** she **writes** well.

8. **Subjects separated by** "either (*plural*) or", "neither (*plural*) nor", "both _____ and", also "all _____ but", take a plural verb, e.g.

   a) **Either** the boys or the girls **are** to blame.

   b) **Neither** the pirates **nor** the sailors **were** afraid of battle.

   c) **Both** Hugh **and** Sam **were** standing.

   d) **All but** James **are** going to the picnic.

   e) **All of** them **but** Grace **are** correct.

Exercises on concord

In each of the sentences below there are groups of two words within brackets. One of the two words is correct, the other wrong. Underline the correct word:

1. Each of the boys (is, are) going on holiday so each of them (has, have) gone to bed early.

2. Everybody (was, were) pleased as each of them (was, were) treated alike.

3. Neither he nor she (want, wants) to go.

4. (Wasn't, Weren't) we sorry when we heard you (was, were) going?

5. One of the men (is, are) married and so he (get, gets) preference.

6. All but William (has, have) behaved well so all but William (get, gets) away early.

7. James, as well as John, (rise, rises) at eight, so James, like John, (is, are) early for work.

8. Neither of the singers (was, were) present.

9. Every little girl (desire, desires) a nice doll.

10. The miller and his wife (is, are) a happy couple.

11. Why (does, do) every one of us (do, does) stupid things at times?

12. Neither of them (has, have) failed as both of them (is, are) right in five sums.

13. The girl, with several others, (was, were) going to school.

14. Both Agnes and Albert (is, are) here tonight.

15. Either Fred or Jean (has, have) made a mistake, so either he or she (is, are) wrong.

16. Not one of the boys (has, have) a knife although not one of the boys (is, are) young.

17. John, like James, (is, are) smaller than Peter.

18. (Is, Are) Frank and Margaret happy, as both he and she (was, were) complaining?

19. All of you but Andrew (is, are) good, so all of you but Andrew (get, gets) a reward.

20. Each of the ladies (is, are) delighted as each of the ladies (receive, receives) a prize.

21. Anybody (is, are) allowed to enter.

22. Every one of us (know, knows) the answers because every one of us (was, were) copying.

23. Nobody (is, are) grumpy at the camp because nobody (is, are) allowed to feel lonely.

24. Arthur, as well as Donald, (is, are) clever, so Arthur, as well as Donald, (has, have) succeeded.

25. The gentlemen and the ladies (was, were) wearing evening dress.

26. Either one or the other (is, are) wealthy as either one or the other (has, have) plenty of money.

27. All of us but David (was, were) on holiday so all of us but David (is, are) feeling relaxed.

28. (Wasn't, Weren't) they pleased when they heard we (was, were) coming?

29. Cecil, as well as Annie, (like, likes) spelling and Cecil, as well as Annie, (hate, hates) arithmetic.

30. Either Flora or Richard (has, have) measles, so either she or he (is, are) in bed.

31. Why (do, does) every one of them do that, when every one of them (know, knows) the arrangements?

Pronouns

There are **personal, relative, interrogative, demonstrative** and **indefinite pronouns**. Pronouns stand **for** (pro-) nouns.

Personal pronouns and some relative and interrogative pronouns have a **nominative** form when they are the subject of a verb, an **objective** form when they are the object of a verb (or preposition) and a **possessive** form. Personal pronouns also distinguish the **first person** (the person(s) speaking, i.e. I or we), the **second person** (the person(s) spoken to, i.e. you) and the **third person** (the person(s) spoken about). So we have:

Personal pronouns

Person	Nominative	Objective	Possessive	Reflexive	(Possessive adjective)
First (Sing.)	I	me	mine	myself	(my)
Second (Sing.)	you	you	yours	yourself	(your)
Third (Sing.)	he	him	his	himself	(his)
	she	her	hers	herself	(her)
	it	it	its	itself	(its)
First (Plur.)	we	us	ours	ourselves	(our)
Second (Plur.)	you	you	yours	yourselves	(your)
Third (Plur.)	they	them	theirs	themselves	(their)

Note 1: The reflexive form is used in two ways, a) reflexive, b) intensive, e.g.

I have cut myself. He blames himself. (reflexive)

I myself was unaware of that. (intensive, emphatic)

Note 2: The reflexives do not have different forms for nominative, objective or possessive. It is wrong to say *hisself* or *theirselves*.

Note 3: A *possessive adjective* simply describes a noun, e.g. *your* pencil.

The *possessive of a pronoun* stands for a noun, e.g.

This pencil is *yours*. (i.e. *your pencil*)

He's a friend of *ours*. (i.e. from among *our friends*)

The **nominative** forms of pronouns must be used for subjects of verbs.

I bought some apples.   *We* saw a large cave.

You will catch a cold.   *They* shouted with joy.

He caught a fish.   *She* sang a song.

The objective forms must be used for objects of verbs or prepositions.

The play bored *me*.   The children left *us*.

The animal stared *at me*.   Go and run *after them*.

Special case – complement of the verb *to be*.

The verb *to be* does not take an object. When we say "That is nonsense", the word *nonsense* is called the complement (or "completion") of the verb *is*.

It *is I* who am the master of my fate.   (*I* is the complement of *is*)

It *was they*, not *we*, who ran away.   (*they*, *we* complements of *was*)

Mistakes are common when *that* is used for *who*, e.g.

It was *them*, not *us*, *that* ran away. (wrong)

In the first sentence we could even have two mistakes:

It is *me* that *is* the master of my fate. (*me*, *is*, both wrong)

Exception: If someone asks "Who is there?" the answer "It is *me*" is now accepted in practice, though "It is I" is the grammatically correct form.

Note: It is not only the simple parts of the verb *to be* which have a complement, e.g.

It *appears to be they* who are refusing.

The above rules – **nominative for the subject** (and for the complement of the verb *to be*), **objective for the object** (of a verb or preposition) – apply also where there is more than one subject or object, e.g. two pronouns, or a noun and a pronoun.

Examples:

She and *I* can't agree.   It suits both *them* and *us*.

It's *you* and *I* who lose.   Between *you* and *me*, he's mad.

Errors:

It's *you* and *me* who lose.   Between *you* and *I*, he's mad.

Other errors to avoid

a)   After *as* and *than*.

(wrong) He is as tall as me.   (correct) He is as tall as *I* (am).

(wrong) He is taller than me.   (correct) He is taller than *I* (am).

Note these sentences, however:

She likes you as much as *me*. ⎱   Both correct. Means "as much as
She likes you more than *me*. ⎰   (more than) she likes *me*".

She likes you as much as *I*. ⎱   Both correct. Means "as much as
She likes you more than *I*. ⎰   (more than) I like you".

b)   Spelling of *its* (pronoun) and *it's*.

Its is the possessive of *it* (with no apostrophe), e.g. This class has forgotten *its* manners.

It's stands for *it is* (or *it has*). The apostrophe denotes omissions, e.g. *It's* dry today, but *it's* been wet recently.

Relative pronouns

A relative pronoun (*who, whom, whose, which, what, that*) joins two parts of a sentence, standing in one part for a noun or pronoun mentioned in the other part, and referring to that noun or pronoun, which is called its **antecedent**, e.g.

Tom is a boy *who* learns fast.   That's a job *of which* I'm proud.

She is a pupil *whom* I taught.   This is the house *that* Jack built.

Was it he *whose* boat sank?   *What* is to be, will be.

Sometimes a relative pronoun is omitted and has to be "understood", e.g.

That's a girl ↑ I taught last year.   The shop ↑ I went to was shut.

Sometimes the pronoun includes its own antecedent, e.g.

Who steals my purse steals trash.   (*who* = *he, who* ...)

What will be, will be.   (*what* = *that, which* ...)

Who, whom refer only to people (singular or plural):

who, the nominative, must be used only for the subject of a verb,

whom, the objective, must always be used for the object of a verb or preposition, e.g. Is there anyone *whom* we can trust? It is wrong to say: Is there anyone *who* we can trust?

Whose, that can refer to people, animals or things, singular or plural.

Which is used to refer to animals and things (singular or plural) but not to people. Its possessive form is either *whose* or *of which*.

What is seldom used as a relative pronoun, though it is common as an interrogative. It is sometimes wrongly used instead of *that*, e.g.

This is the book *what* I lost (wrong).

This is the book *that* I lost (correct).

Interrogative pronouns

Interrogative pronouns (*who? whom? whose? which? what?*) ask a question.

They refer to people, animals and things just as when used as relative pronouns.

It is a common mistake to use *who?* (the nominative form) in sentences where *whom?* (the objective) is required, e.g.

Who do you think I met? (wrong)

Whom do you think I met? (*whom* is the object of *met*) (correct)

Note: *Who* do you think you are? is correct. (*Are* is part of the verb *to be*, which does not take an object.)

Demonstrative pronouns

A demonstrative pronoun (*this, that, these, those*) "points out" what it stands for, e.g.

This is intolerable.   I like *that*.   He is like *that* sometimes.

I prefer *these* to *those*.   *That's* better.   Is it as serious as *that*?

Note 1: *This* and *these*, when opposed to *that* and *those* in a sentence, usually distinguish what is nearer, more recent, or more recently mentioned, from what is more distant in place or time, e.g.

That was nonsense: the truth is *this* ...

Note 2: The words *this, that, these, those* are, of course, also used as (demonstrative) adjectives, when they point out *and* describe a noun in a sentence, or one that is understood, e.g.

This house is bigger than *that* (house).

That is the wrong door. (*door* is understood after *that*)

Indefinite pronouns

An indefinite pronoun stands for some person(s) or thing(s) unspecified, e.g.

Tell me *more*.   You don't know *much*.   *Both* owned up.

Either will do.   *One* must remember.   *None* returned.

Take *any* of them.   Give me a black *one*; I dislike white *ones*.

Note 1: A singular indefinite pronoun should not be referred to as if it were a plural. This is a very common error, e.g.

Everyone must pay *their* fair share (wrong).

Everyone must pay *his* fair share (correct).

Everyone must pay *his* or *her* fair share (correct).

Note 2: Another common error is to switch from the indefinite *one* to another pronoun, e.g.

One must not miss *his* chance (wrong).

One must not miss *one's* chance (correct).

Complete these sentences using the correct word from each pair in brackets:

1. (He, Him) and (I, me) went for a walk.

2. It was (he, him) (who, whom) we saw in the shop.

3. No one believes it was (she, her); everyone thinks it was (I, me).

4. Between (he, him) and (I, me) we ate the whole cake.

5. (She, Her) and (I, me) can go, but you and (he, him) cannot.

6. Jack is not as clever as (he, him) or (I, me).

7. It seems to be (they, them) (who, whom) the police suspect.

8. (Her, She) and you sang very well together.

9. John is much brighter than (he, him) or (I, me).

10. This discovery must remain a secret between you and (I, me).

11. It's not for (we, us) to run after (they, them).

12. It was (he, him) who knew the right answer.

13. (Who, Whom) are (they, them)?

14. (We, Us) lads were at the cinema at the same time as (they, them).

15. Between you and (I, me), I know all about Sue and (she, her).

16. He is almost as big as (I, me) but smaller than (she, her).

17. Her sisters are smaller than (we, us) but she is taller than (I, me).

18. You must choose between (they, them) and (we, us).

19. You and (I, we) could do it, but not you and (he, him).

20. It appears to be (she, her) about (who, whom) you should worry.

21. (She, Her) and (I, me) are twelve years of age.

22. Her cousin is younger than (she, her) or (I, me).

23. Was it (I, me) (who, whom) you saw there?

24. I spoke to (he, him) and (she, her) about (who, whom) to tell.

25. We are certain it was not (he, him) (who, whom) was to blame.

26. It is not (she, her) that I am angry with, but (he, him).

27. (He, Him) I can excuse, but not (they, them).

28. Was it (he, him) or (she, her) who found the purse?

29. (Who, Whom) do you think we met?

30. Anyone (who's, whose) poor shouldn't buy one of (them, these).

31. That's not your pencil. (Its, It's) (mine, mine's).

32. Everyone (what, that) wants a ticket, must bring (their, his) money.

33. Neither he nor she (know, knows) what (they, he or she) (is, are) doing.

34. Let's go, you and (I, me), and see (who's, whose) (there, their).

35. (Who, Whom) were you speaking to?

Conjunctions

A **conjunction** joins words, phrases or sentences together.

There are two main kinds of conjunction:

1. Conjunctions which join similar parts of speech and clauses of equal value, e.g. and, both ... and, but, for, whereas, either ... or, neither ... nor.

   Examples:
   a) The boy **and** the girl hurried home.
   b) The dog was delighted with the bone **and** wagged his tail.
   c) **Both** he **and** his wife went on holiday.
   d) **Both** the driver **and** the man, who was hurt, were questioned.
   e) He was poor **but** honest.
   f) She could write well, **but** she could not do her sums.
   g) I gave him the money, **for** he had earned it.
   h) I am surprised at him **for** he should know better.
   i) He worked hard, **whereas** I did very little.
   j) He thought himself wealthy, **whereas** he was poor.
   k) **Either** my brother **or** his chum knows the place.
   l) **Either** my nephew goes with me **or** he stays at home.
   m) **Neither** James **nor** Mary wants to go.
   n) **Neither** did he come **nor** did he send any excuse.

2. Conjunctions which join principal clauses to subordinate clauses.
   (Included are many adverbs which act as connecting words and therefore become conjunctions.) In order to distinguish the various types of conjunction in this class they are grouped under the appropriate headings below.

Time
Conjunctions are:

| after | before | since | until | till | when | whenever | while | now | that | as |

Examples:
a) **After** the lady opened the door she switched on the light.
b) The man ate a sandwich **before** he boarded the bus.
c) **Since** I have known her we have been firm friends.
d) We will wait here **until** the next train arrives.
e) I cannot say definitely **till** I hear from him.

f) The boys were going to school **when** we saw them.

g) **Whenever** it is possible we shall visit her.

h) **While** there is life there is hope.

i) **Now that** we have finished, let us go home.

j) **As** I was on my way home, I fell.

Place

Conjunctions are:

whence   where   wherever   whither

Examples:

a) He looked back **whence** he had come.

b) Put it **where** he cannot see it.

c) The brooch must be found **wherever** it is.

d) **Whither** thou goest, I will go.

Cause or reason

Conjunctions are:

as   because   lest   since

Examples:

a) **As** he was in a hurry I did not speak to him.

b) We know he was to blame **because** we saw the accident.

c) I was afraid **lest** he should fall.

d) Do not say anything **since** she is frightened.

Concession

Conjunctions are:

although   even if   though   whether ... or   while   as

Examples:

a) **Although** I have written twice, he has not replied.

b) I would not go **even if** I were invited.

c) **Though** the boy had faults I could not but like him.

d) It is the truth **whether** you believe it **or** not.

e) **While** we should condemn vice, we should praise virtue.

f) He could not get the answer, clever **as** he was.

Condition

Conjunctions are:

except that   if   unless

Examples:
a) **Except that** she is a trifle slow, she writes well.
b) Send me word **if** you wish to go.
c) That rascal will do nothing **unless** he is compelled.

Manner or degree

Conjunctions are:

as   as ... as   as if   as though   so ... as   than

Examples:
a) He remained at home **as** he had been ordered.
b) The house is vacant **as** far **as** we know.
c) He speaks **as if** he knows all about it.
d) The animal lay **as though** it were dead.
e) James does not read **so** well **as** Robert.
f) He is taller **than** I am.

Purpose

Conjunctions are:

in order that   lest   so that   that

Examples:
a) They worked hard **in order that** they might finish in time.
b) Take care, **lest** you are hurt.
c) I sent him a letter **so that** he would know.
d) You come to school **that** you may learn.

Consequence

Conjunctions are:

so that   so ... that

Examples:
a) The man spoke loudly **so that** he was easily heard.
b) She is **so** dull **that** she can learn nothing.

Exercises on conjunctions

In the following exercises there are sentences with groups of two words within brackets. One of the two words is correct, the other wrong. Select the correct word.

Time

1. Wait there (how, till) I have finished.
2. He left (before, that) darkness fell.
3. We have remained here (whether, since) you left.
4. (After, Unless) they arrived, they sat down.
5. I can call (however, whenever) it is convenient to you.
6. The exercise will be corrected (before, when) it is finished.
7. His brother waited (except, until) James returned.
8. She read a book (that, while) I wrote a letter.
9. (Now that, Unless) the weather has changed the farmers can expect good crops.
10. (Until, As) he went up the stairs, he stumbled.

Place

1. He went (whence, unless) he could not return.
2. The faithful dog followed his master (lest, wherever) he went.
3. There were many trees (since, where) I sat down.
4. They followed (whither, than) he led them.

Cause or reason

1. (As, Where) we left early, we did not see him.
2. I was afraid to speak (lest, however) he should tell.
3. You ask him, (since, than) you are friends.
4. My uncle was angry (where, because) he was deceived.

Concession

1. The boy is strong and healthy (though, since) he is not tall.
2. (While, Unless) I trust him, I dislike his companions.
3. We will go (how, even if) it rains.
4. (Whether, Where) you like it or not, he will invite you.
5. My cold is much worse (although, whence) I have tried to cure it.

Condition

1. (Except that, Unless) he is sometimes nervous, he manages quite well.
2. She will go (than, if) you ask her.
3. You cannot obtain admission (unless, since) you pay.

Manner or degree

1. You are quite right (while, as far as) I can see.
2. The dog lifted his paw (as though, how) he understood me.
3. She is older (than, since) I am.
4. They did not play (while, so well as) their opponents.
5. The man looked (when, as if) he was a foreigner.
6. I cannot work (as, whence) he can.

Purpose

1. The man put on the light (so that, since) he could read.
2. (In order that, When) they might be in time, they left early.
3. The boy ran quickly (why, lest) he should be left behind.
4. You should go (that, how) you may be cured.

Consequence

1. The dog ran so fast (that, while) he caught the hare.
2. He ran quickly (when, so that) he was in time for tea.

Prepositions

The **preposition** is placed before (pre) a noun or a pronoun. It defines a relationship to the noun or pronoun.

The following list contains the most common prepositions:

about · above · across · after · against · along
amid · amidst · among · amongst · around · at
before · behind · below · beneath · beside · between
betwixt · beyond · by · down · during · except
for · from · in · into · near · of
off · on · over · round · since · through
till · to · towards · under · underneath · until
unto · up · upon · with · within · without

Exercises on prepositions

1. Use the correct prepositions in the blank spaces:
   a) The boy must apologise _____ the lady.
   b) That man is an authority _____ flowers.
   c) The mother was proud _____ her son's success.
   d) He placed the bat _____ the wall.
   e) My cousin put the book _____ the drawer.
   f) It is an exception _____ the rule.
   g) His opinion differs _____ mine.
   h) The man ran _____ the path.
   i) She takes great pride _____ her appearance.
   j) The ball went _____ the window.

2. Supply three suitable prepositions in each sentence:

   a) The pencil lay ⎰ _____ ⎱ the desk.

   b) The man rowed ⎰ _____ ⎱ the river.

   c) The lady sat ⎰ _____ ⎱ the chairman.

3. Underline the prepositions in the following sentences:
   a) I stood on the bridge of the ship.
   b) Above me, I saw a cloudy sky.
   c) The dog leaped over the wall after a ball.
   d) We chased him through a field of hay.
   e) With that ticket you can obtain admission to the show.
   f) My brother received a letter from him.
   g) The farmer stored his hay in a large barn.
   h) Beside the boxes lay several boulders.
   i) The careless boy ran behind the car.
   j) During the year many people were injured in street accidents.

Many people find it difficult to choose the correct prepositions. The following should be read carefully and revised from time to time:

according to	inspired by
afflict with	interfere with
agree to (something)	invasion of
agree with (somebody)	meddle with
aim at	mount an attack on
angry at (something)	opposite to
angry with (somebody)	part from (somebody)
ashamed of	part with (something)
blame for	prevail on
change for (something)	protest against
change with (somebody)	pursuit of
comment on	recoil from
compared with	regard for
complain of	rely on
confer with	similar to
conscious of	suffer from
despair of	tired of (something)
die of	tired with (action)
differ from (opinion)	thirst for (or after)
differ with (somebody)	vexed at (something)
disagree with	vexed with (somebody)
disappointed in (something)	victim of
disappointed with (somebody)	wait for (person, thing)
disgusted at (something)	wait upon (somebody)
disgusted with (somebody)	write about (something)
dislike for	write to (somebody)
divide among (many)	
divide between (two)	
equal to	
filled with	
full of	
good for	
guilty of	
in defiance of	
indignant at (something)	
indignant with (somebody)	

Correction of sentences

The errors below are common. Both grammar and vocabulary are important to a proper grasp of the English language.

There are errors in the following sentences. Rewrite them correctly.

1. She was the oldest of the two sisters.

2. Who did you see at the party?

3. Neither John or James were present.

4. She is not as old as me.

5. The best team won the football match.

6. The books what we read were interesting.

7. Being a fine day I went to the seashore.

8. Who can it be for?

9. He was angry at me for leaving.

10. I am your's truly.

11. I cannot run no farther.

12. John has broke his leg.

13. Hurrah shouted the man.

14. The letter was sent to Mr Jane Brown.

15. The parcel was returned back to the sender.

16. I left home at quarter to 7.

17. The girl said that she done it herself.

18. He returned home as quick as he could.

19. I have forgot to post the letter.

20. "Where is my Boots?" he asked.

21. She hurted her leg.

22. She got a bad accident.

23. There is four books on the table.

24. He went for to get up.

25. The lady bought a comb for the baby with plastic teeth.

26. Between you and I, he is quite wrong.

27. They sung the same song twice.

28. This jacket is wore out:

29. It's no use me working.

30. I intended to have written.

31. I was that tired I could hardly of spoken.

32. The fishermen saw a flock of herring in the sea.

33. Immediately he ran to the injured man.

34. Between you and me we seen many people.

35. I saw a dog with his master which had a long tail.

36. We found the ring belonging to the lady made of gold.

37. A piano was sold to a lady with carved legs.

38. We seen the rascal who stole were ball.

39. There is five books on the table.

40. A man was at the corner and his dog.

41. She and her husband am going.

42. His hair needs cutting badly.

43. Neither of them are tall.

44. Someone's left their books behind.

45. Him and his sister went to the cinema.

46. Me and my friend went to buy a coat for ourselves.

47. It was him you saw.

48. They have did it again.

49. She could not come no quicker.

50. We have never seen none of them.

51. He couldn't remember nothing.

52. He done his work correctly.

53. Is he the tallest of the two?

54. Each of the boys had their books.

55. It was me that broke the window.

56. Which is the cleverest, John or Mary?

57. A more kinder man never lived.

58. I was that breathless I could hardly speak.

59. The animal did not take no notice.

60. Neither of them have been lucky.

61. Me and him went together to the cinema.

62. He took the biggest half.

63. It was a remarkable fine picture.

64. He is worse than me.

65. I seen him go to the theatre.

66. One of the horses were tired.

67. Of the two, I like James best.

68. Give me them oranges.

69. He don't speak very clear.

70. We are quite sure he done it.

71. She sent it to you and I.

72. The man learned him to swim.

73. That answer is different with mine.

74. Neither one or the other is right.

75. She will not stay, I do not think.

76. The lady sings quite nice.

77. He did not except the gift.

78. To who does this belong?

79. The child rose up from the floor.

80. The two brothers divided the apple among them.

The right word in the right place

Although many English words seem interchangeable, it is important to be precise in your selection of which word to use in a given sentence.

1. **Place the following words in the sentences best suited to their use:**
   closed, finished, stopped, completed, concluded, ended.
   a) His watch _____ at six o'clock.
   b) I remember how the story _____.
   c) I have _____ my lessons.
   d) They have _____ the alterations.
   e) The meeting _____ with the National Anthem.
   f) Having enough money, they _____ the fund.

2. **Explain the difference between:**
   learning – teaching, looking – staring, mumbling – bawling,
   striding – galloping, taking – snatching, tapping – battering,
   throwing – hurling, writing – scribbling.

3. **Use the following words (instead of "nice") to describe:**
   agreeable, beautiful, convenient, delicious, enjoyable, fine, good, interesting, pleasant, pretty.

   a _____ garden   a _____ bonnet
   a _____ cake   a _____ walk
   a _____ house   an _____ man
   a _____ day   a _____ train
   an _____ concert   an _____ book

4. **Place the following words in the sentences best suited to them:**
   frowned, mumbled, sang, chuckled, bowed, whispered, listened, smiled.

   She _____ tunefully.   He _____ gleefully.
   She _____ angrily.   She _____ broadly.
   He _____ humbly.   She _____ attentively.
   She _____ indistinctly.   He _____ softly.

5. **Place the following words in the sentences best suited to their use:**
   exclaimed, muttered, answered, said, shouted, explained, whispered, pleaded.

   She _____ that he would come.   She _____ with joy.
   He _____ why he was late.   "Look!" he _____.
   She _____ for mercy.   He _____ under his breath.
   He _____ quietly to his neighbour. "That is so," she _____.

6. **Place the following words in the sentences best suited to them:**
    ate, pulled, charged, slept, bled, crept, strove.

    She _____ furiously.   She _____ greedily.

    He _____ profusely.   He _____ soundly.

    She _____ vigorously.   He _____ manfully.

    She _____ stealthily.

7. Always avoid the use of the word "got". There is usually another word which can be used to better effect.

    Substitute a better word in each of the following sentences:

    a) She got up at eight o'clock.

    b) He got a penny from his mother.

    c) He got his breakfast early.

    d) She got a bad cold yesterday.

    e) She got to the station in time.

    f) He got married last year.

8. **Write in the most suitable word:**

    a) A man who digs for coal is a _____.

    b) I switched on the _____ light.

    c) The _____ holiday is in December.

    d) They sang a Christmas _____.

    e) He was so ill _____ he went to bed.

    f) The postman _____ the letters.

    g) He avoided accidents because he drove very _____.

9. **Place the right words (from** who, whom, whose, which**) in the following sentences:**

    a) That is the boy _____ broke the window.

    b) That is the stone _____ broke the window.

    c) That is the man _____ window was broken.

    d) That is the boy _____ I saw breaking the window.

    e) That is the boy _____ told me that he broke the window.

10. **Give the correct words ending in** *-able*:

    a) A piece of furniture.   f) A telegram from overseas.

    b) A horse's home.   g) Helpless.

    c) Written by Æsop.   h) Land under cultivation.

    d) Can be carried.   i) A carrot.

    e) Diamonds are.   j) Glass things are.

11. **Give a single word for each of the following:**
    a) go away
    b) go back
    c) go down
    d) go forward
    e) go into
    f) go on hands and knees
    g) go out of
    h) go quickly
    i) go slowly
    j) go up

12. **Place the right words (from** no, not, never, none, any**) in the following sentences:**
    a) Did you notice _____ friends there?
    b) _____ have I seen such a display.
    c) We have _____ received _____ of the books.
    d) _____ thank you, I _____ smoke.
    e) We are _____ going there _____ more.
    f) _____ of the boys knew the answer.
    g) _____, he is _____ well enough to eat _____ cakes.
    h) Have you _____ marbles? _____, I have _____.

13. **From the following lengths choose the correct one for each sentence:**
    two millimetres; fifteen centimetres; thirty centimetres; one hundred and eighty centimetres; four metres; seventy metres; six hundred and forty-three kilometres; four thousand eight hundred and twenty-seven kilometres.
    a) The soldier was _____ tall.
    b) My exercise book is _____ wide.
    c) The height of the factory chimney was _____.
    d) The distance from London to Glasgow is about _____.
    e) The string on the parcel was _____ thick.
    f) The distance from Southampton to New York is about _____.
    g) The room was _____ high.
    h) My ruler is _____ long.

14. **Explain the difference between:**

yacht – steamer	car – aeroplane	river – canal	pen – pencil
shoes – boots	chair – sofa	pin – needle	ham – bacon
shadow – reflection	clock – watch	saltfish – cod	hay – straw
picture – sketch	map – plan	ceiling – roof	

15. There are a great many words to describe different ways of walking. For example: A hunter **walked** over the hills. A better word here would be **roved** or **roamed**. In the sentences below replace the word **walked** by a more suitable word from the following list. Any word once used may not be used again, so be careful and **watch your step:**

limped, strode, sneaked, toddled, paced, rambled, tramped, shuffled, plodded, strutted, strolled, stamped, hobbled, marched, sauntered, prowled.

a) The nature lover **walked** through the woods.

b) The lame woman **walked** across the floor.

c) The happy couple **walked** down the lane.

d) The daring knight **walked** into the hall.

e) The tourist **walked** through the art gallery.

f) The soldiers **walked** to the station.

g) Captain Smith **walked** up and down the deck.

h) The cunning thief **walked** into the room.

i) The baby **walked** across the floor.

j) Proud Mrs Brown **walked** on to the platform.

k) The weary farmer **walked** homewards.

l) A gouty old man **walked** down the stairs.

m) The hikers **walked** many a long mile.

n) The angry man **walked** into his office.

o) The burglar **walked** through the house.

p) The sick patient **walked** over to the table.

16. The following may be said to be **the right action at the right time. Tell what immediate action you would take and suggest a cure (if necessary). What would you do?**

a) If you burned your foot.

b) If you lost your way.

c) If you sprained your ankle.

d) If your nose started to bleed.

e) If you noticed an escape of gas in the house.

f) If your sister's dress caught fire.

g) If you found a wallet in the street.

h) If your brother's hand was cut.

i) If you saw smoke coming from a closed shop.

j) If your cousin was stung in the arm.

Addition of clauses

A **clause** is a group of words containing a finite verb. A principal clause can stand alone and make sense, while a subordinate clause cannot. Subordinate clauses can be divided into noun clauses, adjectival clauses and adverbial clauses.

Add a clause to the following and name the kind of clause you add:

1. I saw the lady _____.

2. The little boy said _____.

3. The girl ran quickly _____.

4. _____ when they reached home.

5. I noticed _____ when he rose to speak.

6. We stood on the very spot _____.

7. _____ if you cannot swim.

8. The dog barked _____.

9. The lady _____ was my sister.

10. "Will you let me know _____ ?" she asked.

11. The dog _____ saved the child.

12. We saw the train _____.

13. I hope _____.

14. _____ while they listened.

15. The boy hurt himself badly _____.

16. The man _____ was caught by the police.

17. I saw _____.

18. She bought an umbrella _____.

19. _____ as she spoke.

20. The messenger arrived _____.

21. I watched the man _____.

22. I do not know _____.

23. As the girl approached the house _____.

24. We saw _____ when we returned.

25. _____ if you are ill.

26. "Come to my house _____," she said.

27. I know the child _____.

28. When I came here _____.

29. _____ which cost two pence.

30. My father scolded me _____.

31. The crowd rushed forward _____.

32. The soldiers _____ were trapped in the wood.

33. The unhappy scholar said _____.

34. _____ if you do not send word.

35. The boy lifted the box _____.

36. The man waved frantically _____.

Replacement

A **clause** is a group of words containing a finite verb. A **phrase** is a group of words without a finite verb.

Change the underlined phrases into clauses:

1. He failed <u>through carelessness</u>.
2. <u>On the completion of his task</u> the boy went out to play.
3. He told me <u>of his coming</u>.
4. A man <u>in high position</u> has many responsibilities.
5. She lived in a cottage <u>near the sea</u>.
6. <u>On entering</u> I saw several pictures.
7. The police recovered <u>the stolen property</u>.
8. I was pleased to hear <u>of his success</u>.
9. We do not know <u>his hiding place</u>.
10. The roads <u>leading to the fair</u> were crowded.

Change the underlined clauses into phrases:

1. I am convinced <u>that he is sincere</u>.
2. The child was in bed <u>before the sun had set</u>.
3. His action showed <u>how brave he was</u>.
4. I am certain <u>that you will help me</u>.
5. <u>As I approached</u> I heard a great noise.
6. He met me <u>when I arrived</u>.
7. The man admitted <u>that he was wrong</u>.
8. The girl was absent <u>because she was ill</u>.
9. You cannot succeed <u>unless you work hard</u>.
10. The witness described <u>where the accident took place</u>.

Replace the underlined words with a single word:

1. He wished to see him <u>at once</u>.
2. The concert was <u>put off</u> for a month.
3. The sentry <u>ran away</u> from his post.
4. The concert is held <u>once every year</u>.
5. The army <u>went forward</u> towards the town.
6. The man <u>was sorry</u> for his hasty words.
7. The sun <u>went out of sight</u> behind the clouds.
8. The <u>people who live next door</u> are very kind.
9. They <u>made up their minds</u> to go to the party.
10. That boy is always <u>in time</u>.

Sentences

A **simple sentence** has one finite verb and one idea. A **complex sentence** has one principal clause and one or more subordinate clauses.

Simple to complex

Make each pair of simple sentences into one complex sentence and retain the meaning as far as possible.

(Do not use *and* or *but* or *so*.)

1. a) I have a dog. b) I am very fond of it.
2. a) That is the man. b) He stole my purse.
3. a) I was travelling in a bus. b) It collided with a taxi.
4. a) The boy did not pass. b) His work was badly done.
5. a) I was gazing out of the window. b) I saw a crowd.
6. a) The boy was riding a horse. b) It looked tired.
7. a) The man could hardly walk. b) He carried such a heavy load.
8. a) The book belongs to Jack. b) It is a red one.
9. a) The girl went for the doctor. b) The doctor stayed next door.
10. a) The house was destroyed. b) It was built by Tom's father.
11. a) He works hard at his lessons. b) He wishes to succeed.
12. a) The men were walking quickly. b) The men saw me.
13. a) He heard the sound of music. b) He was passing a church.
14. a) The lady lost the book. b) She was going to the library.
15. a) The man stood at the door. b) The door was open.
16. a) The boy caught a rabbit. b) He took it home.
17. a) The girl fell heavily. b) The girl hurt herself.
18. a) He opened the cupboard. b) He saw many books.
19. a) The lady was careless. b) She lost her purse.
20. a) Mary entered the room. b) The room was brightly decorated.
21. a) A loud peal of thunder came. b) The children were frightened.
22. a) Tom made mistakes in reading. b) He could not see well.
23. a) The teacher praised the boys. b) They had worked well.

24. a) The horse fell.   b) It was pulling a heavy load.

25. a) The man caught a salmon.   b) He took it home.

26. a) The boy has hurt his foot.   b) The boy cannot walk.

27. a) The lady sat in a coach.   b) Four horses drew it.

28. a) The tourist climbed the hill.   b) The hill was steep.

29. a) My sister has a good voice.   b) She sings in the choir.

30. a) The girl found a brooch.   b) She took it to her mother.

31. a) I found a lady's purse.   b) It contained two coins.

32. a) The girl wore a red dress.   b) She sat next to me.

33. a) I visited the little cottage.   b) I was born in it.

34. a) The woman was selling flowers.   b) She stood at the corner of the street.

35. a) I went to see my cousin.   b) His home was in the country.

36. a) The man was poorly clad.   b) I gave him money.

Complex to simple

Change the following complex sentences into simple sentences and retain the meaning as far as possible:

1. He is a man who is very intelligent.
2. We heard the news that he was saved.
3. I can tell you how old he is.
4. The woman lives in a house which is very big.
5. Maria spoke to the soldier who was wounded.
6. The boy lost his ticket because he was careless.
7. I shall speak to him when he arrives.
8. The child found a ring which was very valuable.
9. He asked me where I lived.
10. Can you tell me which way the wind is blowing?
11. I saw him when the clock struck five.
12. We all believed the story that the traveller told.
13. Huge telescopes are used by people who study the stars.
14. As soon as the sun rose the soldiers resumed their march.
15. He asked for the book in which one finds the meanings of words.
16. I admit that I have made a mistake.

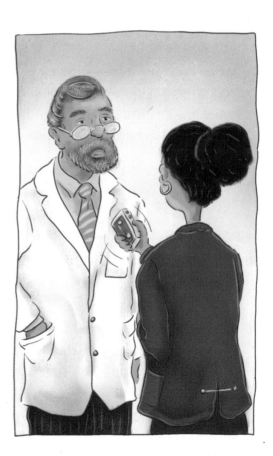

Alphabetical order

Putting words in alphabetical order means following the order of letters as they appear in the alphabet.

Practically all books containing lists have the words arranged in the order of the letters of the alphabet:

1. By the **first** letters of the words.
2. When the first letters are the same, the words are arranged according to the **second** letters.
3. When the first two letters are the same, the words are arranged according to the **third** letters. And so on.

Examples:

1. **By the first letter:**

   anchor, bicycle, height, machine, physical, seized, vehicle, yacht.

2. **When the first letters are the same:**

   absence, accurate, aeroplane, ancient, attention, autumn, awkward.

3. **When the first two letters are the same:**

   thatch, their, thimble, though, through, thumb, thyme.

Exercises on alphabetical order

1. Place the following words in alphabetical order:
   vegetable, official, judgement, colonel, extremely, necessary, language, immediately.

2. Rearrange the following words in dictionary order:
   beginning, brooch, biscuit, business, byre, bough, balance, blossom.

3. Place the following words in alphabetical order:
   complaint, cocoa, correct, coffee, condition, coarse, collection, course.

4. Rearrange the following words in dictionary order:
   dismissed, disguise, displayed, disaster, district, discovery, disobeyed, disease.

Apostrophes

The possessive case of a noun is shown by a mark (') known as an apostrophe.

In **singular** nouns it is shown by '*s*, e.g. Mary's bag, the animal's foot, Keats's poems, Burns's songs. *Exception*: it may however be shown by the **apostrophe only** (') to avoid awkward-sounding double or treble *s* endings, e.g. Moses' anger, Jesus' words, Aristophanes' comedies.

In the **plural** it is shown in **two** ways:

a) **By the apostrophe only** (') when the plural ends in -*s* or -*es*, e.g. the boys' books, the ladies' coats.

b) **By the apostrophe and *s*** ('*s*) when the **plural does not end in *s***, e.g. the children's toys, the men's hats.

Singular possessive	Plural possessive
the girl's dress	the girls' dresses
the lady's bag	the ladies' bags
the boy's pencil	the boys' pencils
a day's work	seven days' work
the man's pipe	the men's pipes
the woman's glove	the women's gloves
the child's clothes	the children's clothes

Exercises on apostrophes

Correct the following sentences by putting in the apostrophes:

1. The boys pencil lay on the floor.
2. The ladies coats were in the cloakroom.
3. My cousins hand was badly hurt.
4. The mens boots were covered with mud.
5. The childs doll fell into the pond.
6. I saw that the object was a womans glove.
7. The register lay on the teachers desk.
8. He looked very smart in page-boys uniform.
9. It took several hours hard work to repair the damage.
10. In the window was a special display of babies clothes.
11. The childrens books were left in my uncles house.
12. The girls dress was torn by a neighbours dog.
13. My fathers wallet was discovered in the thieves den.
14. A ducks egg is generally cheaper than a hens.
15. Mr Smiths watch is five minutes slower than Mr Browns.

The apostrophe as a contraction

When the apostrophe is used to contract words it is placed where the letters have been omitted, e.g.

all's	all is	o'clock	of the clock
can't	cannot	o'er	over
couldn't	could not	shan't	shall not
'cross	across	she'll	she will
didn't	did not	shouldn't	should not
doesn't	does not	that's	that is
don't	do not	there's	there is
hasn't	has not	they'll	they will
haven't	have not	we'll	we will
he'd	he would	we've	we have
he'll	he will	whate'er	whatever
he's	he is	where'er	wherever
I'll	I will	whosoe'er	whosoever
I'd	I would	who've	who have
I'm	I am	won't	will not
isn't	is not	wouldn't	would not
it's	it is	you'll	you will
I've	I have	you're	you are

Exercises on the apostrophe as a contraction

1. Insert the apostrophe where it should be:

   tis, neednt, youll, Halloween, souwester, Ive, twas, neer, oclock, dont.

2. Write the following sentence making use of the apostrophe as a contraction:

   We will probably arrive at seven of the clock if there is a convenient bus.

Capital letters

Capital letters are used:
1. to begin sentences
2. to begin special names
3. to begin direct speech
4. to begin words in titles
5. to begin lines of poetry
6. to begin words of exclamation
7. to begin words He, Him, His, if they refer to God or Christ
8. to write the word "I".

Beginning sentences

One day a girl was playing on a busy street. Her ball rolled into the middle of the road and she ran after it. At that moment a car came dashing round the corner. A passer-by saw the girl's danger and ran quickly to her aid. Fortunately he saved her from serious injury.

Special names

Jean Miller and her brother David are expected to arrive by Concorde from New York on Tuesday, November 30th, St Andrew's Day.

Direct speech

A man said to his friends, "If you manage to solve the puzzle, send me the answer." His companions replied, "We will send you our solution before the end of the week."

Titles

The famous collection of Indian animal stories called *The Jungle Book* was written by Rudyard Kipling.

Lines of poetry

I wandered lonely as a cloud
That floats on high o'er vales and hills,
When all at once I saw a crowd,

A host of golden daffodils,
Beside the lake, beneath the trees,
Fluttering and dancing in the breeze.

Exclamation

"Oh!" shouted the boy, "I have hurt my finger." "Indeed!" exclaimed his father, "You are lucky to get off so lightly."

Reference to God or Christ

After Jesus had preached to the multitude He proceeded on His way to Jerusalem.

The pronoun "I"

He advised me to travel by bus but I told him that I preferred to travel by rail.

Punctuation

By correct punctuation we mean the proper use of:

capital letters, comma (,), full stop or period (.), quotation marks (" "), exclamation mark (!), question mark (?) and apostrophe (').

Punctuate the following sentences:

1. What time is it asked the traveller
2. His father said where is your brothers knife
3. My friend exclaimed what a lovely view
4. He has gone to school said his sister in a quiet voice
5. The child suddenly shouted look
6. Oh cried the boy i have hurt my finger
7. Come here said his mother all right replied the boy
8. The man asked have you seen the hammer yes replied his companion it is on the table
9. A boy said to his friend are you going to the cinema no replied the other im on my way home
10. When i return said the girl to her father will you tell me the story of the shipwreck very well he answered but dont be too long at your aunts

Diminutives

The word **diminutive** implies smallness relative to someone or something else, either in physical size, or age, or in importance.

booklet	cygnet	cigarette	laddie	chicken
bracelet	eaglet	epaulette	lassie	kitten
goblet	islet	kitchenette	bullock	maiden
leaflet	leveret	pipette	hillock	cubicle
ringlet	locket	rosette	damsel	icicle
rivulet	owlet	statuette	morsel	particle
baronet	pocket	duckling	satchel	lambkin
circlet	darling	nestling	gosling	mannikin
sapling	seedling	dearie	globule	napkin
coronet	briquette	girlie	molecule	piglet

Small quantities

Many words exist in English to convey the idea of smallness; here are some examples of the words and how they are used.

air	a breath, puff, whiff		paper	a scrap
bread	a crumb, crust, morsel		rain	a drop, spot
butter	a pat, nut		salt	a grain, pinch
colour	a dab, tint, touch		sand	a grain, particle
corn	an ear		smoke	a wisp
dirt	a particle, speck, spot		snuff	a pinch
energy	an ounce		soot	a smut, speck
flowers	a nosegay, posy		straw	a wisp
food	a morsel, particle, scrap		sugar	a grain, spoonful
glass	a splinter, fragment		tea	a pinch, spoonful
grass	a blade, tuft		time	a moment, second
hair	a lock, strand		water	a drop, sip
light	a beam, glimmer, ray		wind	a puff, whiff
liquid	a drop, sip		wood	a chip, splinter

For reference

Reference material is the material to which you refer when you are looking for a particular type of information.

To find	Look at
1. the address of a person	directory
2. the meaning of a word	dictionary
3. the day and date of the month	calendar
4. the position of a place	atlas
5. a list of priced goods or books	catalogue
6. a telephone number	telephone directory
7. the time of a train or bus	timetable
8. record of a ship's progress at sea	log
9. record of attendance	register
10. record of personal daily events	diary
11. collection of photos and autographs	album
12. extracts from books and papers	scrapbook
13. record of recent happenings	newspaper or the internet
14. facts regarding days of the year	almanac
15. a fictitious tale	novel
16. a life story	biography
17. material regarding living creatures	book on zoology
18. material regarding plants	book on botany
19. material regarding the stars	book on astronomy
20. material regarding the Earth's crust	book on geology

Proverbs

Proverbs are popular sayings expressed in a clever, brief manner.

1. A bad workman always blames his tools.
2. Absence makes the heart grow fonder.
3. A bird in the hand is worth two in the bush.
4. A cat may look at a king.
5. A drowning man will clutch at a straw.
6. A fool and his money are soon parted.
7. A friend in need is a friend indeed.
8. A hungry man is an angry man.
9. All's well that ends well.
10. An apple a day keeps the doctor away.
11. A miss is as good as a mile.
12. A penny saved is a penny gained.
13. A rolling stone gathers no moss.
14. A stitch in time saves nine.
15. As well be hanged for a sheep as a lamb.
16. A small leak will sink a great ship.
17. As the twig is bent so the tree's inclined.
18. As you make your bed so must you lie in it.
19. Better late than never.
20. Birds of a feather flock together.
21. Charity begins at home.
22. Cut your coat according to your cloth.
23. Discretion is the better part of valour.
24. Don't carry all your eggs in one basket.
25. Don't count your chickens before they are hatched.
26. Early to bed, early to rise, makes a man healthy, wealthy and wise.
27. Empty vessels make most noise.
28. Enough is as good as a feast.
29. Every cloud has a silver lining.

30. Every dog has its day.

31. Faint heart never won fair lady.

32. Fair exchange is no robbery.

33. Fine feathers make fine birds.

34. Fine words butter no parsnips.

35. Fire is a good servant but a bad master.

36. First come, first served.

37. Forbidden fruit tastes sweetest.

38. Good wine needs no bush.

39. Great minds think alike.

40. Great oaks from little acorns grow.

41. Habit is second nature.

42. Half a loaf is better than no bread.

43. He laughs best who laughs last.

44. He who pays the piper calls the tune.

45. Hunger is the best sauce.

46. Imitation is the sincerest form of flattery.

47. In for a penny, in for a pound.

48. It's a long lane that has no turning.

49. It's an ill wind that blows nobody any good.

50. Laugh and grow fat.

51. Least said, soonest mended.

52. Leave well alone.

53. Let not the pot call the kettle black.

54. Let sleeping dogs lie.

55. Listeners hear no good of themselves.

56. Children should be seen and not heard.

57. Look after the pence, and the pounds will look after themselves.

58. Look before you leap.

59. Love laughs at locksmiths.

60. Make hay while the sun shines.

61. Misery makes strange bedfellows.

62. More haste, less speed.

63. Necessity is the mother of invention.

64. New brooms sweep clean.

65. None but the brave deserve the fair.

66. None so deaf as those who will not hear.

67. No news is good news.

68. No smoke without fire.

69. Once bitten twice shy.

70. One good turn deserves another.

71. One man's meat is another man's poison.

72. One swallow does not make a summer.

73. Out of sight, out of mind.

74. Out of the frying pan into the fire.

75. Penny wise, pound foolish.

76. Pride goes before a fall.

77. Robbing Peter to pay Paul.

78. Sauce for the goose is sauce for the gander.

79. Set a thief to catch a thief.

80. Silence gives consent.

81. Spare the rod and spoil the child.

82. Speech is silver, silence is golden.

83. Still waters run deep.

84. The early bird catches the worm.

85. Too many cooks spoil the broth.

86. Truth will out.

87. Two heads are better than one.

88. Unity is strength.

89. We never miss the water till the well runs dry.

90. Where there's a will there's a way.

91. When the cat's away the mice will play.

Colloquialisms

Colloquialisms are expressions used in everyday conversation.

Expression	Meaning
the apple of one's eye	somebody specially dear
armed to the teeth	completely armed
a wet blanket	a discouraging person
dead beat	exhausted
in the same boat	in the same circumstances
carried away	highly excited
a chip off the old block	very like one's father or mother
all ears	paying close attention
at a loose end	having nothing to do
off form	not so capable as usual
good for nothing	useless
a son of a gun	a likeable rogue
hard of hearing	almost deaf
hard up	short of money
hard hit	seriously troubled
ill-used	badly treated
lion-hearted	of great courage
at loggerheads	quarrelling
the man in the street	an ordinary man
up to the mark	good enough, well enough
an old salt	an experienced sailor
a peppery individual	a cranky, hot-tempered person
a pocket Hercules	a small but strong man
at rest	dead
a rough diamond	a person of real worth but rough manners
silver-tongued	plausible and eloquent
golden-voiced	pleasing to hear
out of sorts	not well
on the level	honest
stuck up	conceited
thick in the head	stupid

Expression	Meaning
beside oneself	out of one's mind (with anger, grief)
heavy-eyed	sleepy
under a cloud	in trouble or disfavour
down in the mouth	in low spirits
down on one's luck	in ill-luck

General colloquial expressions

Here are some general colloquial expressions to use in everyday conversation.

Expression	Meaning
weigh anchor	lift the anchor
keep up appearances	maintain an outward show
have a bee in one's bonnet	be obsessed with an idea
put one's best foot forward	do best possible
sweep the board	take all
make no bones about it	be plain and outspoken
burn the candle at both ends	overdo work and play
have one's heart in one's boots	be very despondent
have one's heart in one's mouth	be frightened
bury the hatchet	make peace
make a clean breast of	confess
have a feather in one's cap	have something to be proud of
set one's cap at	try to captivate
throw in the cards	give up the struggle
throw in the towel	give up the struggle
cast up	reproach
show a clean pair of heels	escape by running
pull up short	stop suddenly
wait till the clouds roll by	await more favourable circumstances
turn one's coat	change one's principles or allegiance
give the cold shoulder	show indifference or ignore
throw cold water on	discourage
cut a dash	be very showy
lead a dance	delude
lead up the garden path	deceive by hiding real intention
keep a thing dark	hide something
keep one's distance	stay aloof
lead a dog's life	have a wretched life
draw the line	fix the limit
keep one's powder dry	be ready or prepared
pull wool over the eyes	deceive

Expression	Meaning
make both ends meet	manage financially
face the music	meet the worst
sit on the fence	avoid taking sides
put one's foot in it	cause embarrassment by word or action
fall foul of	come up against
get into hot water	get into trouble
take French leave	go without permission
play the game	act fairly
hit below the belt	act unfairly
hold one's tongue	keep silent
blow one's own trumpet	boast
hit the nail on the head	be right
bite the dust	fall to the ground, be defeated
kick over the traces	throw off control
knock on the head	stop suddenly
turn over a new leaf	conduct oneself better
pull someone's leg	hoax
tell it to the Marines	no one believes that
go through the mill	undergo suffering
put the cart before the horse	start at the wrong end
make the mouth water	cause to desire
sling mud	slander
nip in the bud	stop at an early stage
send someone packing	dismiss quickly
play fast and loose	act carelessly
keep the pot boiling	keep an activity going
rain cats and dogs	rain very heavily
raise one's dander	anger
mind your Ps and Qs	be careful about your behaviour
smell a rat	be suspicious
take a rise out of	fool
rub up the wrong way	irritate by opposing
get into hot water	get into trouble
turn the tables	reverse a result
back chat	be impudent
ride the high horse	be snobbish, arrogant
let the cat out of the bag	tell what should be kept secret

Expression	Meaning
send to Coventry	ignore as a punishment
haul over the coals	scold or punish
take the bull by the horns	act despite risks
strike while the iron is hot	act without delay
take forty winks	sleep
chew the fat	argue
act the goat	behave foolishly
live from hand to mouth	live in hardship
hang one's head	feel ashamed
turn up one's nose	scorn deliberately
play with fire	tempt serious trouble
swing the lead	avoid work purposely
blaze the trail	lead the way
come a cropper	fail, fall to earth

Popular phrases

The meaning of each of the phrases below is not always obvious. However, it is worth learning them because they give everyday language colour and life.

Explain what is meant by the following phrases:

horse play   back to the wall   for a lark   from pillar to post

a fine kettle of fish   a bird's eye view   as the crow flies   a busman's holiday

a stiff upper lip   no flies on him   a blind alley   a cat on hot bricks   a dead cert

a cock and bull story   a far cry   with flying colours   a flash in the pan

a fly in the ointment   the lion's share   on the nail   not a patch on

pins and needles   bats in the belfry   a storm in a teacup   by hook or by crook

Doubles

Doubles are used in speech to give greater emphasis.

1. **By repetition of actual word:**

   again and again, by and by, neck and neck, out and out, over and over, round and round, so and so, such and such.

2. **By repetition of meaning:**

   beck and call, ways and means, far and away, puff and blow, null and void, stuff and nonsense, fast and furious, odds and ends, rant and rave, lean and lanky, out and away, hue and cry, bawl and shout, old and grey.

3. **By alliteration (words beginning with the same letter):**

   humming and hawing, kith and kin, might and main, part and parcel, safe and sound, hale and hearty, spick and span, alas and alack, time and tide, rack and ruin, rough and ready, one and only.

4. **By opposites:**

   this and that, thick and thin, on and off, great and small, in and out, high and low, come and go, give and take, one and all, ups and downs, here and there.

5. **By words of similar sound:**

   high and dry, fair and square, out and about, wear and tear.

6. **By related words:**

   heart and soul, hip and thigh, tooth and nail, body and soul, root and branch, lock and key, hammer and tongs, hole and corner, head and shoulders, hand and foot.

7. **Other examples:**

   all and sundry, fast and loose, fits and starts, hard and fast, free and easy, rough and tumble, habit and repute, over and above, touch and go, time and again.

Exercises on doubles

Place the following phrases in the most suitable sentences:

again and again, lock and key, spick and span, puff and blow, odds and ends.

1. The police placed the man under _____.
2. He polished his boots until they were _____.
3. She tried to do it _____.
4. The child had gathered many _____.
5. The stout man began to _____ with exertion.

Colours

The following are the colours of the rainbow:

| violet | indigo | blue | green | yellow | orange | red |

There are other colours, such as: white, black, purple, brown, pink, grey and crimson.

Sometimes we refer to things as being:

blood-red	bottle-green	brick-red	cinnamon-brown	coal-black
milk-white	nut-brown	pea-green	primrose-yellow	rose-pink
ruby-red	russet-brown	sea-green	shell-pink	sky-blue
slate-grey	snow-white			

Often we make use of "colour" words in everyday speech, e.g.

1. I saw it in **black and white**.
    I saw it in writing (or print).

2. I am in his **black books**.
    He is displeased with me.

3. The man **looked blue**.
    The man looked as if he was depressed.

4. He was in a **blue funk**.
    He was in great terror.

5. He had **blue blood** in his veins.
    He was of aristocratic descent.

6. The **green-eyed monster** caused him to strike his friend.
    Jealousy caused him to strike his friend.

7. He was a **greenhorn** at the game.
    He was raw and inexperienced at the game.

8. The fellow was **yellow at heart**.
    The fellow was really a coward.

9. He was born **in the purple**.
    He was of royal birth.

10. The business was a **white elephant**.
    The business was a failure.

11. It was a **red letter day** for me.
    It was a notable and fortunate day for me.

12. She **saw red** when she got the bill.
    She was very angry when she got the bill.

Exercises on colours

Complete the following sentences:

1. The old colonel was purple with _____.
2. The bully turned white with _____.
3. The little child was blue with _____.
4. His rival was green with _____.
5. The pages of the book were yellow with _____.

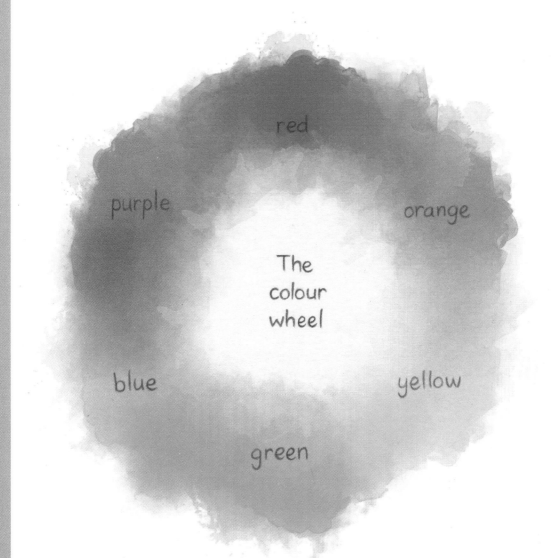

red

purple

orange

The
colour
wheel

blue

yellow

green

Our five senses

Most people have five senses by which they are able to see, hear, smell, taste and touch.

Sight   Sight is the ability to observe or perceive by the <u>eye</u>.

Hearing   Hearing is the ability to listen or perceive by the <u>ear</u>.

Smell   Smell is the ability to detect odour or perceive by the <u>nose</u>.

Taste   Taste is the ability to detect flavour in the mouth or perceive by the <u>tongue</u>.

Touch   Touch is the ability to detect objects by contact or perceive by <u>feeling</u>.

Derivations

A **root** is a word in its first and simplest form. A word may be built up or have its meaning changed by an addition at either end. The addition at the beginning is known as a **prefix**, e.g. dis-agree. The addition at the end is known as a **suffix**, e.g. paint-er.

Roots

Word	Meaning	Examples
aqua	water	aquatic, aqueduct
audio	I hear	audible, audience, audit
capio	I take	capable, captive, capture
centum	a hundred	centenarian, century
clamo	I shout	clamour, proclaim, exclaim
creo	create	creation, creature
curro	I run	courier, current, excursion
decem	ten	December, decimal
dico	I say	edict, dictation, verdict, dictator
duco	I lead	produce, reduce, introduce
facio	I make	fact, factory, perfect
finis	an end	final, infinite
fortis	strong	fort, fortify
homo	a man	homicide, human
impero	I command	empire, emperor, imperial
liber	free	liberal, liberty
malus	bad	malady, malice, maltreat
manus	hand	manual, manufacture, manuscript
mitto	I send	missile, mission, remittance
navis	a ship	navigate, navy
octo	eight	octagon, octave, October
pello	I drive	expel, propel, repel
pendeo	I hang	depend, pendant, suspend
pes	a foot	pedal, pedestrian, quadruped
planus	level	plain, plan, plane
plus	more	plural, surplus
porto	I carry	export, import, porter, transport
poto	I drink	poison, potion

Word	Meaning	Examples
primus	first	primer, primitive, Prime Minister
rego	I rule	regal, regent, regiment
rota	a wheel	rotate, rote, rotund
ruptus	broken	eruption, interruption, rupture
scribo	I write	scripture, describe, manuscript
specio	I see	aspect, prospect, spectacles
teneo	I hold	contain, retain, tentacles
unus	one	unit, unity, union
vanus	empty	vanish, vanity, vain
venio	I come	adventure, prevent, venture
video	I see	provident, visible, vision
vinco	I overcome	convince, victory
voco	I call	revoke, vocal, voice
volvo	I roll	evolve, revolve, volume

Prefixes

Prefix	Meaning	Examples
a-	on	afloat, ashore, aloft
a-, ab-, abs-	away, from	avert, absolve, abstract
ad-, ac-, ar- (etc.)	to	adhere, accept, arrive, assume, attract
ante-	before	antecedent, anteroom
anti-	against	antagonist, anti-aircraft
bi-, bis-	two, twice	bicycle, biped, bisect, biscuit
circum-	round	circumference, circuit
com-, con-	together	comparison, competition, contact
contra-	against	contrary, contraband, contradiction
de-	down	depress, descend, describe
dif-, dis-	apart, not	different, disagree, disappear
ex-	out of	exhale, export, extract
fore-	before	forecast, forenoon, foretell, foresee
im-, in-	in, into	import, include
in-	not	incapable, inhuman
inter-	between	international, interrupt, interval
mis-	wrong	misdeed, misjudge, mistake
ob-	against	object, obstruction

Prefix	Meaning	Examples
post-	after	postpone, postscript, post-war
pre-	before	predict, prepare, pre-war
pro-	forth	proceed, produce
re-	back	retake, return, retrace
sub-	under	submarine, subway
trans-	across	transfer, transport, transpose
un-	not, without	unfit, unknown, unpaid, unsafe
vice-	instead	vice-captain, viceroy

Suffixes

Suffix	Meaning	Examples
-able, -ible	capable of being	movable, edible, incredible
-ain, -an	one connected	chaplain, publican
-ance, -ence	state of	repentance, existence
-ant	one who	assistant, servant
-el, -et, -ette	little	satchel, locket, cigarette
-er, -eer, -ier	one who	baker, engineer, furrier
-ess	the female	goddess, princess, waitress
-fy	to make	glorify, purify, simplify
-icle, -sel	little	particle, morsel
-less	without	careless, guiltless, merciless
-ling	little	codling, gosling, darling
-ment	state of being	merriment, enjoyment
-ock	little	hillock, bittock
-oon, -on	large	saloon, balloon, flagon
-ory	a place for	dormitory, factory
-ous	full of	famous, glorious, momentous

1. Underline **the root parts** of the following words and give their meanings:
   century, December, factory, manual, navigate, suspend, pedal, export, describe, tentacles.

2. Underline **the prefixes** in the following words and give their meanings:
   anteroom, bicycle, circumference, contradict, forenoon, international, postscript, submarine, transport, unknown.

3. Underline **the suffixes** in the following words and give their meanings:
   heiress, explorer, simplify, duckling, careless, edible, attendant, decorator, courageous.

General knowledge

We acquire general knowledge from the world around us, from other people, newspapers, the internet, books and other media. A good general knowledge is very useful in adult life.

In the following list many questions can be answered by one word. Wherever possible, do so.

1. A boy who frightens weaker boys.
2. A number of soldiers.
3. The men and women who work on a ship.
4. Children in a school.
5. A man who protects sheep.
6. The low ground between two hills.
7. A place where pupils are educated.
8. A ship which travels below the surface of the sea.
9. A place for storing a car.
10. A small leaf.
11. A mammal that can fly.
12. A field in which fruit trees grow.
13. An instrument for measuring time.
14. From what do we make butter?
15. A man who makes things out of wood.
16. A fertile place in the desert.
17. A man who pretends to be good.
18. A person who is always boasting.
19. A stream which flows into a river.
20. A hundred years.
21. Name an instrument for telling direction.
22. What are the steps of a ladder called?
23. Name two spotted animals.
24. A doctor who performs operations.
25. What is the front part of a ship called?
26. Headgear worn by some inhabitants of India.
27. A place where beer is made.
28. What is daybreak sometimes called?
29. A man who draws and paints.
30. Fish with the bones taken out.
31. A shallow crossing in a river.

32. Two creatures which see well in the dark.

33. What is the meaning of plume?

34. Name any American money.

35. Girl or woman who serves at table.

36. A person who by desire lives alone.

37. What do we call the breaking of a bone?

38. Name two shellfish.

39. What is the flesh of a sheep called?

40. The first meal of the day.

41. The city which has the Eiffel Tower.

42. Name of metal container for oil.

43. Place in which photographs are taken.

44. A place where people are buried.

45. Another name for a policeman.

46. Name three "string" instruments.

47. Name the imaginary line round the middle of the Earth.

48. An instrument which measures heat and cold.

49. From what do we make cheese?

50. Name the five human senses.

51. What kind of fish is a kipper?

52. Type of footwear in hot countries.

53. A place where whisky is made.

54. The most accurate kind of clock in the world.

55. Name three infectious diseases.

56. What lights must a steamer show at night?

57. Name two striped animals.

58. Goods carried out of a country.

59. A place where birds are kept.

60. Person who gives life in a good cause.

61. The air surrounding the Earth.

62. A person who saves and hoards money.

63. A religious song.

64. How does a fish breathe in water?

65. Name the colours of the rainbow.

66. What is the small top room of a house?

67. Which is Britain's fiercest wild bird?

68. What is the national dress of Scotland?

69. A three-sided figure.

70. A place where aeroplanes are kept.

71. Meaning of "The Seven Seas".

72. A vessel for holding flowers.
73. What is the meaning of steed?
74. Name the patron saint of England.
75. A person who cannot hear or speak.
76. A room on board a ship.
77. A soldier with three stripes on each arm.
78. A person who takes the place of another.
79. How many legs does a fly have?
80. Name four kinds of tree.
81. A place where iron goods are made.
82. Name four great deserts.
83. Name three animals living mostly in water.
84. A man who does tricks with cards.
85. Water which has turned into gas.
86. The young that hatch from insect eggs.
87. What is the flesh of a pig called?
88. Scottish loch in which there is said to be a monster.
89. Goods taken into a country.
90. A place where leather is made.
91. Another name for a donkey.
92. Machine which makes electricity.
93. What is milk-fat called?
94. What is wind?
95. What is ackee?
96. What is a tripod?
97. What is the flesh of the deer called?
98. Name for smuggled goods.
99. What language was spoken by the ancient Romans?
100. A place where chickens are hatched.
101. What is an astronaut?
102. What are the primary colours?
103. Of what wood is a cricket bat made?
104. Name quick ways of sending messages.
105. What is the Milky Way?
106. What was Guyana formerly called?
107. Place where gas is stored.
108. Who were the Caribs?
109. Explain lbw.
110. What is a boneshaker?
111. Which is the lightest common metal?

112. What does NASA do?

113. Where is the longest wall in the world?

114. What is the capital of Cuba?

115. A place where fish are kept.

116. Who was Man Friday?

117. What is a mimic?

118. A rotating device that pushes along a ship or aircraft.

119. Give the common name for the spine.

120. What is a planet?

121. What is meant by scuttling a ship?

122. Give the motto of the (Boy) Scout Association.

123. In which country do people wear wooden shoes?

124. What is a grotto?

125. Name three "wind" instruments.

126. A place where you can lunch for payment.

127. Where is the Empire State Building?

128. What do scuba divers do?

129. What is the basin of a river?

130. What is capital punishment?

131. Which planet is closest to the sun?

132. Who was Long John Silver?

133. A picture that shows the bones inside the body.

134. What side is starboard?

135. Who is the patron saint of Scotland?

136. What is meant by "crossing the line"?

137. What are the Antipodes?

138. Who was the British Prime Minister in 2003?

139. In the northern hemisphere, which month contains the longest day?

140. Which country is called Erin?

141. Name two "percussion" instruments.

142. What is a song for two called?

143. Name an oil used as a medicine.

144. How many in a "baker's dozen"?

145. What is a centenarian?

146. Instrument used for drawing circles.

147. Another name for a jungle.

148. An aircraft that can fly without an engine.

149. What is the longest-living tree in the world?

150. Which insect makes honey?

151. Name any animal covered with spines.

152. When is the signal "SOS" used?

153. When is Christmas Day?

154. What is a cutlass?

155. Where were the Olympic Games first held?

156. How many teeth does an adult person have?

157. Who is the patron saint of Ireland?

158. What do we call water when solid?

159. What is a loom?

160. Name any "pouched" animals.

161. What is a fjord?

162. An instrument for seeing tiny objects.

163. Who was David Livingstone?

164. In the northern hemisphere, which month contains the shortest day?

165. Lemons, oranges and grapefruit are all _____ fruits.

166. Name five common garden flowers.

167. Group of countries including Sweden, Norway and Denmark.

168. What is a storey?

169. Which animal is called the "King of Beasts"?

170. Who is the patron saint of Wales?

171. A funny drawing of general interest.

172. Where did the Incas live?

173. Another name for an airman.

174. What is a burnous?

175. What is a bed on board a ship called?

176. How many sides does a hexagon have?

177. In which country are the Great Lakes found?

178. What is a quadruped?

179. Which animal covers great distances without water?
180. What is a hobo?
181. Group of animals to which apes, monkeys and humans belong.
182. What is a rickshaw?
183. What kind of vegetable are cassavas, yams and sweet potatoes?
184. A number of icebergs.
185. City famous for high buildings.
186. Another name for an aeroplane.
187. What is a weather satellite?
188. Name the insect which carries malaria fever.
189. What is the yellow part of an egg called?
190. Who was Mars?
191. When is a person said to be myopic?
192. Name given to a sailor's map.
193. What is the skin of the orange called?
194. Crabs, lobster and prawns are all _____.
195. Another word meaning remedy.
196. Soldiers on horseback.
197. What is meant by a bird's-eye view?
198. Who is a sheik?
199. What are the ingredients used for making tea?
200. Name of the bowl-shaped opening at the top of a volcano.
201. How is bronze made?
202. Another name for a learner.
203. What is the Aurora Borealis?
204. American dog used to pull sledges.
205. Stone bowl used to make flour.
206. What is a Thermos flask?
207. Another name for a way out sign above a door.
208. Name the largest planet in our solar system.
209. The top of a hill or mountain.
210. What is coral?
211. Meaning of umpire.
212. Rope used by a cowboy.
213. What is meant by walking in Indian file?
214. To what country does a "Yankee" belong?
215. Another name for a village.
216. What is a banshee?
217. Name given to soldiers on foot.
218. A place from which stone or slate is obtained.

219. A pocket case for holding money and documents.
220. Another name for an inn.
221. What is the white of an egg called?
222. Give another word meaning salary.
223. What is meant by walking abreast?
224. What is a coyote?
225. What is peculiar about a Manx cat?
226. From what do we obtain coffee?
227. What is a cog wheel?
228. Name an animal which chews the cud.
229. What is a cataract?
230. Which letters are vowels?
231. Name any beast of prey.
232. Why was Peter Pan different from other children?
233. What is a lunar probe?
234. What is a life buoy?
235. From what tree would you expect acorns to fall?
236. Which animal has a tail called a brush?
237. What is a gondola?
238. From what do we obtain cider?
239. What is a carnivorous creature?
240. Remedy for stings.
241. Name the ABC islands.
242. What is the handrail for a stair called?
243. What is a nuclear power station?
244. A clergyman's house is called a _____.
245. What is savannah?
246. What is the capital of England?
247. Where is the "New World"?
248. Name an animal with a very long neck.
249. What is veal?
250. Medical supplies used to treat cuts.
251. Which is the biggest ocean in the world?
252. Name an insect which appears to carry a lamp.
253. What is a nightmare?
254. Which creatures have antlers?
255. What is a hod?
256. What were the kings of the Ancient Egyptians called?
257. Name given to a young tree.
258. What is the middle part of an apple called?

Fastenings

Fastenings hold or attach one object to another.

Name things fastened by the following:

belt	glue	mortar	solder
bolt	handcuffs	nail	staple
braces	harness	padlock	strap and buckle
brooch	hawsers	paste	string
button	hinge	peg	strut
cable	hook and eye	pin	tack
cement	lace	putty	thread
chain	latch	rivet	twine
clip	lock	rope	zip
cord			

Useful information

Most of these facts are unlikely ever to change.

The **principal languages of the world** are as follows (arranged according to the number speaking each): Chinese, Spanish, English, Arabic, Hindi, Bengali, Portuguese, Russian, Japanese and German.

The **continents** are: Europe, Asia, Africa, North America, South America, Antarctica and Australia.

The **oceans** are: Atlantic, Pacific, Indian, Arctic and Southern.

The **largest islands** (other than the continents) are: Greenland, New Guinea, Borneo, Madagascar and Baffin Island.

The **greatest lakes** are: Caspian Sea (Asia: borders Russia and Iran among others), Lake Superior (North America), Victoria Nyanza (Central Africa), Aral Sea (Asia: between Kazakstan and Uzbekistan), Lake Huron (North America) and Lake Michigan (North America).

The **highest mountains of the world** are: Mt Everest, Mt Godwin-Austin (K-2), Mt Kangchenjunga, Mt Lhotse and Mt Makalu. These are all located in the Himalaya and Karakoram mountain ranges.

The **longest rivers** are: Missouri-Mississippi (United States), Amazon (Brazil), Nile (Egypt), Yangtse (China), Lena (Russia), Zaire (Central Africa), Niger (West Africa) and Yenesei (Russia).

Some of the **largest cities of the world** are: Tokyo (Japan), Mexico City (Mexico), New York (USA), São Paulo (Brazil), Delhi (India), Shanghai (China), Beijing (China), Seoul (South Korea) and Cairo (Egypt).

Various countries – the peoples – their main languages

Country	People	Language
Australia	Australians	English, Aboriginal languages
Bangladesh	Bangladeshis	Bengali
Belgium	Belgians	Flemish, French
Bulgaria	Bulgarians	Bulgarian
Canada	Canadians	English, French
China (People's Rep.)	Chinese	Chinese
Czech Republic	Czechs, Slovaks	Czech
Denmark	Danes	Danish
Egypt	Egyptians	Arabic
England	English	English
Finland	Finns	Finnish
France	French	French
Germany	Germans	German
Greece	Greeks	Greek
Netherlands	Dutch	Dutch
Hungary	Hungarians	Hungarian
India	Indians	Hindi, English
Iran	Iranians	Farsi
Ireland (Eire)	Irish	English, Gaelic
Israel	Israelis	Hebrew, Arabic
Italy	Italians	Italian
Jamaica	Jamaicans	English
Japan	Japanese	Japanese
Kenya	Kenyans	Swahili, English
Malawi	Malawians	CiCewa
Mexico	Mexicans	Spanish
New Zealand	New Zealanders	English, Maori
Nigeria	Nigerians	Yoruba, Hausa, Ibo
Pakistan	Pakistanis	Urdu
Poland	Poles	Polish
Portugal	Portuguese	Portuguese
Russia	Russians	Russian

Origin of certain place names

Africa was so named by the Romans after the Afri tribe of Tunisia.

America is named after Amerigo Vespucci, who explored parts of the coastline of the New World, shortly after its discovery by Columbus.

Asia the largest continent, takes its name from the district behind Smyrna in Turkey. We sometimes refer to the eastern part of the continent as the "orient" (land of the rising sun).

Australia means the "southern continent". National emblems – kangaroo, emu, mimosa.

Europe some say it was named Eref by the Phoenicians, meaning "The land of the setting sun" and sometimes referred to as the "occident". Others say it was named after Europus, a town in Macedonia.

Canada from the Native American word "Kannata", meaning "a number of settlers' huts". National emblems – maple leaf, beaver.

China (The Chinese people seldom use this name but generally refer to the province concerned.) The word is said to have come from "Tsin", the ruler who built the Great Wall of China. National emblems – dragon, plum blossom.

England land of the Angles, who invaded and conquered South Britain in the 5th century. National emblems – lion, rose, bulldog.

France (Old name Gaul – land of the Gauls.) Present name from the Franks, who later conquered the country. National emblems – lily, cock, eagle.

Germany "Germanus" (neighbour), a Roman word borrowed from the Gauls. Germans call their country "Deutschland". National emblems – eagle, corn flower.

India the land through which the River Indus has its course. National emblems – elephant, star, lotus, jasmine.

Ireland (Gaelic name – Eire) – land of the Irish tribe. National emblems – shamrock, harp.

Italy (= vitalia) – means "cattle or pasture land". National emblems – eagle, lily, laurel wreath.

Japan The Japanese always use the word "Nippon" and both mean "The land of the rising sun". National emblems – chrysanthemum, rising sun.

New Zealand (New Sea Land) – so named by a Dutch explorer after Zealand – a part of the Netherlands. National emblems – kiwi, fern.

Nigeria Nigeria was named after the River Niger.

Russia land of the tribe of Russ. National emblems – an eagle with two heads.

Scotland (Old name Caledonia). Present name from the Scots, a north of Ireland tribe, who invaded and gradually became masters of the whole country. National emblems – lion, thistle.

South Africa (see "Africa"). National emblems – springbok, real yellowwood.

Spain English form of the word "Hispania" or "España". The name comes from "Shapan" (rabbit land), as the Phoenicians found the country overrun with these animals. National emblems – red carnation, pomegranate.

USA (see "America"). National emblems – eagle, buffalo, golden rod.

Turkey land of the Turks. National emblem – star and crescent.

Wales (Old name Cymru – land of the Cymry tribe). Present name is derived from Anglo-Saxon word meaning "land of the foreigner". National emblems – leek, daffodil, dragon.

Various countries and their capitals

Country	Capital	Country	Capital
Albania	Tirana	Kenya	Nairobi
Argentina	Buenos Aires	Netherlands	Amsterdam
Australia	Canberra	New Zealand	Wellington
Belgium	Brussels	Nigeria	Abuja
Belize	Belmopan	Norway	Oslo
Brazil	Brasilia	Pakistan	Islamabad
Bulgaria	Sofia	Poland	Warsaw
Canada	Ottawa	Portugal	Lisbon
China	Beijing	Rumania	Bucharest
Colombia	Bogotá	Russia	Moscow
Cuba	Havana	Scotland	Edinburgh
Czech Republic	Prague	South Africa	Cape Town
Denmark	Copenhagen	Spain	Madrid
Egypt	Cairo	Sri Lanka	Colombo
England	London	Sweden	Stockholm
France	Paris	Switzerland	Berne
Germany	Berlin	Thailand	Bangkok
Greece	Athens	Trinidad	Port of Spain
Hungary	Budapest	Turkey	Ankara
India	New Delhi	Uganda	Kampala
Ireland	Dublin	United States	Washington DC
Italy	Rome	Uruguay	Montevideo
Jamaica	Kingston	Venezuala	Caracas
Japan	Tokyo	Zimbabwe	Harare

Currencies of various countries

Argentina	peso, centavo	Luxembourg	euro, cent
Australia	dollar, cent	Mexico	peso, centavo
Belgium	euro, cent	Netherlands	euro, cent
Canada	dollar, cent	New Zealand	dollar, cent
China	yuan, fen	Nigeria	naira, kobo
Denmark	krone, øre	Poland	zloty, grosz
Egypt	pound, piastre	Portugal	euro, cent
France	euro, cent	Russia	rouble, kopeck
Germany	euro, cent	South Africa	rand, cent
Greece	euro, cent	Spain	euro, cent
India	rupee, paisa	Switzerland	franc, centime
Italy	euro, cent	Turkey	lira, juru
Japan	yen, sen	United States	dollar, cent
Kenya	shilling, cent	Vietnam	dong

Exercises on useful information

1. With which **country** or **people** do you associate each of the following?

Ali	Foreign Legion	moccasins	scimitar
Balmoral	furs	mummies	shamrock
Beefeater	gaucho	onions	sombrero
beret	Hans	oranges	spaghetti
bolas	heather	ostrich	tea
boomerang	ice cream	Pablo	tigers
butter	John Bull	reggae	tomahawk
cheese	kangaroo	reindeer	tulips
chop-sticks	kilt	rickshaw	turban
chrysanthemum	lariat	rising sun	Uncle Sam
clogs	leek	rose	vodka
corn flower	lotus flower	salmon	watches
cowboy	macaroni	sandals	whisky
daffodil	Marianne	sari	windmills
fez	midnight sun		

2. With which **countries** do you associate the following beasts of burden?

camel, dog, donkey, dromedary, elephant, horse, llama, mule, ox, reindeer, yak

3. Who use (or used) the following kinds of boats?

canoe, coracle, dhow, galleon, gondola, junk, kayak, sampan

4. What **national** names are often attached to the following?

Example: Kenyan coffee. **Scotch** broth.

baths, carpets, cheese, curry, onions, noodles, rum, sausage, stew, tea

5. Who use (or used) these weapons?

boomerang, cutlass, harpoon, tomahawk, truncheon

6. In what **country** would you be if your journey was called a:
   a) safari, b) mush, c) hajj, d) trek?

7. In which **countries** might men have each of the following names?
   Angus MacDonald, Tom Smith, Evan Jones, Patrick O'Neil, Chang Wu, Fritz Schmidt, Ivan Petrovitch, Juan Caballero, Pierre Sablon, Hans Brinker.

8. In which **town and country** is each of the following situated?
   Cleopatra's Needle, Colosseum, Eiffel Tower, Leaning Tower, Nelson's Column, Pyramids, The Golden Gate, The Golden Horn, The Houses of Parliament, The Kremlin, The Statue of Liberty, The Sphinx, The Taj Mahal, The Bridge of Sighs, The White House, The Vatican

9. In which **countries** are the following mountains situated?
   Blue Mountains, Cotopaxi, Mt Everest, Fujiyama, Mt Blanc, Kilimanjaro, Table Mountain, The Rockies, Uhuru Peak, Vesuvius

10. With which **countries** are the following famous people associated?

    Nelson Mandela, Captain Cook, Bob Marley, George Washington, Jomo Kenyatta, Mao Zedong, Ned Kelly, Indira Gandhi, Duke Ellington, Diego Maradona, Pele, Florence Nightingale, Mother Teresa, Stalin, Hitler, Aretha Franklin, Joan of Arc, Julius Caesar, Martin Luther King, Napoleon, Kemal Ataturk, Mozart, Fidel Castro, Yasser Arafat, Peter the Great, General De Gaulle

11. To what **countries** do the following names (seen on foreign stamps) apply?

    Argentina, Belgique, Danmark, Eire, Suomi, France, Deutschland, Nederland, Italia, Norge, Polska, Romania, España, Sverige, Suisse or Helvetia

The wonders of the world

In olden times travellers who visited foreign lands generally brought back amazing tales of the wonderful sights they had seen on their journeys. The most famous of these sights became known as the Seven Wonders.

1. The pyramids of Egypt.
2. The Hanging Gardens of Babylon.
3. The tomb of Mausolus at Halicarnassus.
4. The temple of Artemis (Diana) at Ephesus.
5. The Colossus at Rhodes.
6. The statue of Zeus (Jupiter) at Olympia.
7. The Pharos Lighthouse at Alexandria.

Of the above **Seven Wonders of the Ancient World** only the great pyramids of Egypt survive today.

In the Middle Ages people considered that there existed other sights quite as wonderful and named the following:

1. The Colosseum of Rome.
2. The Leaning Tower of Pisa.
3. The Catacombs of Alexandria.
4. The Great Wall of China.
5. Stonehenge.
6. The Porcelain Tower of Nanking.
7. The Mosque of St Sophia in Constantinople (Istanbul).

All of these **Wonders of the Middle Ages** (some of which are much older than the Middle Ages) still stand or have remains which can still be seen.

Today it would be impossible to make a completely satisfactory list of Seven Wonders as we have all seen or heard of many amazing man-made structures and scientific marvels. Under these two headings the following are remarkable enough to be included in any list of **Wonders of the Modern World**:

Man-made structures

1. Simplon Tunnel.
2. The skyscrapers of New York (USA).
3. The Boulder Dam of Colorado (USA).
4. The Panama Canal (Central America).
5. The Golden Gate Bridge at San Francisco (USA).
6. The Taj Mahal at Agra (India).
7. North Sea Oil drilling rigs and production platforms.

Scientific marvels

1. Internal combustion engine.
2. Concorde.
3. Space travel.
4. Anaesthetics.
5. Heart surgery.
6. Bio-engineering.
7. Radio.
8. Radar.
9. Fibre-optics communication.
10. Television.
11. Lasers.
12. Computers.

Science vocabulary

1. doctor's "listening" instrument — stethoscope
2. magnifies tiny objects — microscope
3. makes distant objects look bigger, nearer — telescope
4. measures heat and cold — thermometer
5. measures heat of the body — clinical thermometer
6. indicates the weather — barometer
7. measures gas or electricity used — meter
8. helps the voice to carry — megaphone
9. picks up sound for sending out again — microphone
10. carries messages by wire — telephone
11. carries sound without use of wires — radio
12. carries messages by wire across the sea — cable
13. takes photographs — camera
14. takes photographs through the body — X-rays
15. glasses used for bettering the eyesight — spectacles
16. instrument used for telling time — watch
17. tells if a thing is horizontal — spirit-level
18. tells if a thing is vertical — plumb-line
19. gives direction — compass
20. a sailor's map — chart
21. a ship which can travel below the water — submarine
22. attracts iron — magnet
23. makes electricity — dynamo / alternator
24. ship's engine which works by steam — turbine
25. a machine for measuring time — clock
26. measures angles in surveying — theodolite
27. instruments for drawing circles — compasses
28. releases over-pressure of steam — safety-valve
29. machine used in business for letter-writing — computer / word processor
30. causes the spark in motor engine — magneto / distributor

Did you know?

Sound travels 1.6 km in 5 seconds.

Light travels approximately 300,000 km in 1 second.

Light takes 8 minutes to reach the Earth from the Sun.

36 km per hour is equal to 10 m per second.

1 litre of water weighs 1 kg.

1 nautical mile is 1.85 km.

Spelling lists

It is important to learn to spell while you are young. Good spelling will stand you in good stead for the rest of your life.

Home	People	Body	Food
attic	adult	ankles	bacon
bolster	ancestors	arteries	biscuits
cellar	aunt	exercise	bread
chimney	babies	forehead	butter
curtains	children	heart	cheese
cushion	comrade	knees	chocolate
detergent	cousin	knuckles	cocoa
hearth	friend	limbs	coffee
kitchen	guest	lungs	margarine
lobby	hostess	muscles	marmalade
mattress	maiden	nostrils	mutton
meter	nephew	shoulder	porridge
mirror	niece	skeleton	pudding
parlour	orphan	skull	sago
pillow	parents	stomach	salmon
poker	relation	thigh	sandwich
saucer	uncle	throat	sausages
scullery	visitor	tongue	steak
towel	widower	veins	sugar
tumbler	youth	wrist	venison

Clothing	Trades	Travel	Travel
braid	butcher	aeroplane	electricity
cloak	carpenter	airship	engine
costume	chemist	balloon	express
cotton	clothier	bicycle	fares
flannel	doctor	brakes	gangway
gabardine	draper	carriage	guard
garments	druggist	coach	helicopter
jacket	engineer	cruise	label

Clothing	Trades	Travel	Travel
linen	grocer	locomotive	skis
lingerie	journalist	luggage	sledge
muslin	lawyer	machine	sleigh
petticoat	mason	parcel	steerage
satin	mechanic	passengers	steward
stocking	plumber	pedals	tourist
trousers	purveyor	pier	tramway
tweed	riveter	platform	traveller
velour	sawyer	purser	tunnel
velvet	sculptor	saloon	vehicle
waistcoat	tailor	seaplane	wagons
woollen	wright	signal	whistles

Land	Sea	Sky	Coast
cape	billows	altitude	bathing
cliff	breakers	astronomy	beach
continent	breakwater	atmosphere	billows
country	channel	cloudy	breeze
headland	crest	comet	cliffs
hillock	fjord	creation	cockles
island	harbour	crescent	costume
marsh	inlet	dawn	diving
mound	lagoon	eclipse	herring
mountain	lake	hazy	lobster
pampas	loch	heavens	mussels
peninsula	ocean	horizon	pier
plain	river	midnight	rowing
prairie	rivulet	planet	seaweed
precipice	sea	solar	shingle
summit	streamlet	sunset	swimmer
tundra	torrent	telescope	view
valley	tributary	twilight	whelks
veldt	trough	universe	winkles
volcano	waves	zenith	wreck

Time	Sport	School	Hospital
ancient	badminton	calendar	accident
annual	bowls	ceiling	casualty
August	boxing	chalk	chloroform
autumn	cricket	composition	disease
century	fencing	copies	doctor
Christmas	football	cupboard	fever
dawn	golf	dictation	infection
Easter	hockey	easel	massage
era	polo	grammar	medicine
February	putting	history	ointment
gloaming	rounders	hymns	operation
January	rugby	interval	paralysis
minutes	shinty	partition	physician
modern	skating	pastels	plaster
punctual	sleighing	pencil	poison
Saturday	sprinting	picture	sterilise
September	swimming	poetry	surgeon
Thursday	tennis	pupil	thermometer
Tuesday	wrestling	scholar	tonic
Wednesday	yachting	teacher	ward

Mammals	Mammals	Mammals	Dogs
ape	dromedary	jaguar	Airedale
armadillo	elephant	kangaroo	Alsatian
badger	ferret	leopard	bloodhound
bat	fox	lion	borzoi
bear	gazelle	llama	bulldog
beaver	giraffe	lynx	collie
buffalo	goat	mole	dachshund
bull	gorilla	mongoose	Dalmatian
camel	hare	monkey	greyhound
cat	hedgehog	moose	Newfoundland
cow	hippopotamus	mouse	Pekinese
deer	horse	mule	pointer
dog	hyena	otter	Pomeranian
donkey	jackass	ox	poodle

Mammals	Mammals	Mammals	Dogs
panther	reindeer	tiger	retriever
pig	seal	walrus	Saint Bernard
porcupine	sheep	weasel	setter
puma	skunk	whale	sheepdog
rabbit	squirrel	yak	spaniel
rat	stoat	zebra	terrier

Birds	Birds	Birds	Fish
albatross	hawk	redshank	cod
blackbird	heron	robin	dogfish
budgerigar	jackdaw	rook	eel
canary	kingfisher	sandpiper	flounder
chaffinch	lapwing	seagull	flying-fish
cormorant	magpie	skylark	goldfish
corncrake	moorhen	snipe	haddock
crane	nightingale	sparrow	halibut
crow	owl	starling	herring
cuckoo	oyster-catcher	stork	mackerel
curlew	parrot	swallow	pike
dipper	partridge	swan	plaice
duck	peewit	swift	roach
eagle	pelican	tern	salmon
falcon	penguin	thrush	shark
finch	pheasant	turkey	skate
flamingo	pigeon	vulture	sole
gannet	plover	wagtail	swordfish
goose	puffin	woodpecker	trout
guillemot	raven	wren	whiting

Trees	Flowers	Flowers	Insects
apple	aster	daffodil	ant
ash	bluebell	dahlia	bee
beech	buttercup	daisy	beetle
birch	carnation	dandelion	bug
cedar	chrysanthemum	forget-me-not	butterfly
chestnut	crocus	foxglove	centipede

Trees	Flowers	Flowers	Insects
elm	geranium	peony	cricket
fir	gladiolus	poppy	daddy-long-legs
hawthorn	honeysuckle	primrose	dragonfly
larch	hyacinth	queen-of-the-meadow	earwig
lime	iris	rhododendron	flea
maple	lilac	rose	fly
oak	lily	snowdrop	gnat
olive	lily-of-the-valley	sunflower	grasshopper
palm	lotus	sweet pea	locust
pine	lupin	thistle	louse
poplar	marigold	tulip	midge
rowan	narcissus	violet	mosquito
sycamore	orchid	wallflower	moth
yew	pansy	waterlily	wasp

Fruit	Vegetables	Minerals	Liquids
apple	bean	aluminium	acid
apricot	beetroot	brass	alcohol
banana	cabbage	bronze	beer
blackcurrant	carrot	coal	brine
bramble	cauliflower	copper	cider
cherry	celery	gold	cocoa
currant	cucumber	granite	coffee
damson	garlic	iron	lemonade
gooseberry	leek	lead	milk
grape	lettuce	marble	oil
lemon	onion	mercury	paraffin
melon	parsley	nickel	petrol
orange	parsnip	platinum	port
peach	pea	radium	sherry
pear	potato	silver	tea
pineapple	radish	slate	turpentine
plum	rhubarb	steel	vinegar
raspberry	sprout	sulphur	water
strawberry	tomato	tin	whisky
tomato	turnip	zinc	wine

General tests

Test 1

1. Break down the following sentence into clauses:

   When the girl returned from **London** she told **her** father **that** she had seen a **grizzly** bear which **performed** tricks in the circus.

2. Parse the words printed in **bold** type in Question 1.

3. a) State the feminine of:

   waiter, bachelor, horse, manservant, husband.

   b) Give the plural of:

   knife, child, penny, sheep, piano.

4. Insert the names of the creatures:

   The _____ brays.   The _____ hoots.

   The _____ grunts.   The _____ chatters.

   The _____ croaks.   The _____ bleats.

   The _____ barks.   The _____ neighs.

   The _____ howls.   The _____ trumpets.

5. Correct the following sentences:

   a) He said that you done it.

   b) She is the biggest of the twins.

   c) It was me that took the pencil.

   d) The man went for to get the book.

   e) A piano was sold to the lady with carved legs.

Test 2

1. Select from each of the following sentences the subordinate clause and tell its kind and relation:

   a) The cottage where Burns was born stands **near** Ayr.

   b) He told **me secretly** where he was going.

   c) The **soldiers** slept where they found a **resting** place.

2. Parse the words printed in **bold** type in Question 1.

3. Supply the missing words:

Example: As sharp as a needle.

As black as _____.   As fast as _____.

As meek as _____.   As happy as _____.

As brave as _____.   As keen as _____.

As sweet as _____.   As steady as _____.

As cold as _____.   As fit as _____.

4. a) Give the objective case of:

   I, he, you, we, they.

   b) Give the past tense of:

   does, hides, writes, sings, bites.

5. Change the clauses set in **bold** type into phrases:

   a) The child was in bed **before the sun had set**.

   b) Flowers will grow **where conditions are suitable**.

   c) Remember to write **when you arrive**.

   d) I saw her **when the clock struck four**.

   e) I am convinced **that he is sincere**.

Test 3

1. Break down the following sentence into clauses:

   When the gentleman arrived at his home he **discovered** that he had left **his** umbrella in the **train**.

2. Parse the words printed in **bold** type in Question 1.

3. Write down the comparatives and superlatives of:

   many, hot, evil, famous, little.

4. a) Name the homes of the following:

   horse, hare, traveller, eagle, bee.

   b) By adding a prefix form words opposite in meaning to:

   possible, secure, welcome, use, legal.

5. Change all singulars into plurals and verbs into past tense:

   a) The rabbit runs from the dog.

   b) The girl wears a blue dress.

   c) The sailor swims to his ship.

   d) He has a sharp knife.

   e) I keep my bird in a cage.

Test 4

1. Read the following sentence and then answer the questions below:
   When I heard that the man was seriously injured I resolved to help him in every way possible.
   a) Write out the adverbial clause.
   b) What parts of speech are: I, seriously, resolved, possible?
   c) What part of the verb is **to help**?
   d) What number is **him**?
   e) What is the subject of **was injured**?
   f) Write down the preposition in the sentence.

2. a) Form nouns from:
      introduce, loyal, revive, ready, broad.
   b) Form adjectives from:
      parent, reason, fortune, poet, winter.

3. Use any five of the following words (one for each sentence) to form short sentences:
   instinct, obstinate, traditional, respectively, occurrence, standard, respectable, resolved.

4. Put the correct prepositions in the blank spaces:
   a) The boy was told not to meddle _____ the pencils.
   b) She felt ashamed _____ herself.
   c) The man took great pride _____ his garden.
   d) The child has been lost _____ Thursday.
   e) He hurried home _____ school.

5. What is meant by saying a person is:
   a) hard up   f) at rest
   b) hard of hearing   g) lion-hearted
   c) stuck up   h) ill-used
   d) dead beat   i) an old salt
   e) all ears   j) out of sorts?

Test 5

1. Break down the following sentence into clauses:
   We were **thoroughly** alarmed when information reached us that the **train** in **which** our friends were travelling had been involved in a **serious** accident.

2. Parse the words printed in **bold** type in Question 1.

3. a) Some Christian names have popular short names, e.g.
   Robert – Bob, Catherine – Kate.
   Give the short names for:
   Albert, Christina, Frederick, Patrick, Elizabeth.
   b) In which countries do the following peoples live?
   Dutch, Maoris, Inuit, Greeks, Welsh.

4. Punctuate and insert capital letters where necessary:
   do you think said my friend in a whisper that theres a chance of escape certainly i replied.

5. Insert the following phrases in their sentences:
   rack and ruin, thick and thin, head and shoulders, safe and sound, out and out.
   a) The ship reached harbour _____.
   b) The man was an _____ rascal.
   c) She is _____ taller than her brother.
   d) Later through foolishness he went to _____.
   e) The soldiers would follow their general through _____.

Test 6

1. Read the following sentence and then answer the questions below:
   When the man reached the garden gate he noticed that the old house in which he was born was in ruins.
   a) What parts of speech are:
   garden, that, which, was, ruins?
   b) Write out the principal clause.
   c) Write out the subordinate adjective clause.
   d) Name the kind of sentence.

2. In the following list of words, one word seems out of place. Underline the word you consider is wrong:
   coat, hat, gloves, curtains, stockings.
   blue, yellow, ruler, green, pink.
   saw, envelope, plane, hammer, chisel.
   anchor, rope, string, twine, cord.
   needle, pin, scissors, thimble, spoon.

3. Where would you look to find:
   The address of a person?
   The position of a place?

The meaning of a word?

The day and date of the month?

Something which happened the previous day?

4. Give the past tense and past participle of the following verbs:
   break, fly, hide, ring, swim.

5. What is meant in each of the following proverbs?
   a) Let sleeping dogs lie.
   b) Too many cooks spoil the broth.
   c) Once bitten twice shy.

Test 7

1. Add a clause and name the kind of clause you add:
   a) We ran for shelter _____.
   b) When the rain stopped _____.
   c) Mary told him _____.
   d) The cunning fox _____ could not be caught.

2. Correct the following sentences:
   a) Walk as quick as possible.
   b) He has forgot the address.
   c) Neither Tom or I can swim.
   d) This end of the rope is the thickest.
   e) The time was quarter past 9.

3. Make a noun from **strong**.
   Make a verb from **courage**.
   Make an adjective from **obey**.
   Give the opposite of **poverty**.
   Give a similar word to **mute**.

4. Medal, board, loose, waist, hoping, lose, meddle, hopping, bored, waste.
   Fill in the blank spaces of the following sentences, using the most suitable words from the above list:

   The teacher told the little boy not to _____ with the _____ as it had a _____ hinge. The child went over to the _____ paper bin _____ to find his pencil.

5. The following is written in the **singular number** and **present tense**. Change it into **plural number** and **past tense**.

   I have a cousin who stays on that little farm. He knows that I like to come here on my holiday.

Test 8

1. Read the following sentence carefully and then answer the questions below.

   When the soldiers reached the city walls they saw that the town which the enemy had completely ruined had been deserted for some time.

   a) Give the case and relation of: town, which, walls.

   b) What parts of speech are: city, that, reached, enemy, for, some?

   c) Write out the subordinate adverbial clause.

2. a) Give the opposites of:

   seldom, visible, praise, export, advance.

   b) Give similar words to:

   enemy, purchase, feeble, perceive, conceal.

3. Your answer in each case should be one word:

   a) A person who explores under the sea.

   b) Water which has turned into gas.

   c) Name of metal container for oil.

   d) A place where birds are kept.

   e) A vehicle that conveys the sick or injured to hospital.

4. Join the following ten words in pairs so that they form five sensible compound words:

   head, black, gentle, dust, egg, bin, ache, board, cup, man.

5. Complete these proverbs:

   a) A stitch in time _____.

   b) A bird in the hand _____.

   c) Birds of a feather _____.

   d) A rolling stone _____.

   e) First come _____.

6. Give the meaning of:

   a.m., Co., BBC, PO, p.m., MP, UK, AD, USA, JP.

Test 9

1. Add a clause and name the kind of clause you add:

   a) The boys ran away _____.

   b) The lady _____ was my sister.

   c) The man saw _____ when he returned.

   d) _____ before the child arrived.

2. a) State the masculine of:

    witch, duck, aunt, vixen, wife.

    b) Give the singular of:

    loaves, armies, roofs, sheep, feet.

3. Use each of these verbs – frowned, mumbled, sang, chuckled, bowed, whispered, listened, smiled – once only to complete the following sentences:

    a) He _____ tunefully.

    b) He _____ angrily.

    c) He _____ humbly.

    d) He _____ indistinctly.

    e) He _____ gleefully.

    f) He _____ broadly.

    g) He _____ attentively.

    h) He _____ softly.

4. A number of sheep together is called a **flock**.

    What name is given to a number of:

    ships, insects, herring, angels, thieves, wolves, chickens, pups, players?

5. Make each pair of sentences into one sentence without using **and** or **but** or **so**.

    a) The house was destroyed. It was built by Tom's father.

    b) He works hard at his lesson. He wishes to succeed.

    c) The men were walking quickly. The men saw me.

    d) He heard the sound of music. He was passing the church.

    e) The lady lost the book. She was going to the library.

Test 10

1. Read the sentences below and then answer the questions:

    Our little hut was situated among the high mountains near the River Dee. Along the banks lay green pastures to which deer came frequently in winter.

    a) What case is **hut**?

    b) What kind of noun is **Dee**?

    c) What part of speech is **our**?

    d) Parse **among**.

    e) What is the subject of **lay**?

    f) Parse **frequently**.

    g) What tense is **came**?

    h) What part of speech is **which**?

    i) What gender is **deer**?

    j) What part of speech is **high**?

2. a) Form adjectives from: affection, nature, attraction, pride, value.

    b) State opposites of: success, arrive, often, sense, entrance.

3. Make sentences, one for each word, showing the correct use of:
   coarse, course, root, route, rode, rowed, currant, current.

4. Rewrite the following correctly:
   a boy said to his friend where are you going james oh replied the other i'm on my way home.

5. Give one word in place of each:
   a) A fertile place in the desert.
   b) A person who by desire lives alone.
   c) An instrument for measuring heat and cold.
   d) A person who looks on the bright side of things.
   e) A stream which flows into a river.

Test 11

1. a) Make a sentence containing **that he would come** as a noun clause.
   b) Make a sentence containing **which he bought** as an adjective clause.
   c) Make a sentence containing **when he reached the station** as an adverbial clause.

2. Give the:
   plural of **ox**
   feminine of **tiger**
   word for a young **swan**
   word for the traditional home of an **Inuit**
   adverb from **danger**.

3. Put in the suitable words in the spaces below:
   Example: Little is to **big** as **dwarf** is to **giant.**
   Sheep is to **mutton** as **pig** is to _____.
   High is to **low** as _____ is to **down.**
   Soldier is to _____ as **sailor** is to **navy.**
   _____ is to **herring** as **school** is to **whales.**
   Bee is to **hive** as **cow** is to _____.

4. Change the following **complex sentences** into **simple sentences**:
   a) There is a boy who is very proud.
   b) He spoke to me while he was passing.
   c) The girl who is intelligent gave the right answer.
   d) The man bought a boat which is very big.
   e) We received word that he was rescued.

5. With which countries do you associate the following famous people?

Robert the Bruce _____   George Washington _____

Stalin _____   Napoleon _____

Captain Cook _____   De Valera _____

David Livingstone _____   Jomo Kenyatta _____

Lloyd George _____   Gandhi _____

Test 12

1. Read the sentence and then answer the questions below:

When the boys who were playing in the park heard the school bell ringing loudly they were afraid that they would be late.

What parts of speech are:

who, park, loudly, school, that?

What part of the verb is **playing**?

What is the case of **bell**?

What is the number of **boys**?

What is the subject of **heard**?

What is the gender of **they**?

2. a) Give the gender of:

lion, cousin, table, waitress, friend.

b) Give words similar in meaning to:

lair, disappear, inside, empty, quickly.

3. Give the names of the shops where you would buy the following:

fruit	_____	spectacles	_____	flowers	_____
hats	_____	milk	_____	newspapers	_____
fish	_____	meat	_____	sweets	_____
tobacco	_____				

4. Change all nouns and verbs into plural:

a) The lady is very beautiful.   d) The valley is broad.

b) Is the salmon fresh?   e) The goose makes a loud noise.

c) The son-in-law is ill.

5. Who use the following articles?

hoe	_____	anvil	_____	safety-lamp	_____
solder	_____	palette	_____	hod	_____
awl	_____	spanner	_____	cleaver	_____

Test 13

1. In the following sentences there are groups of two words within brackets. One of the two words is correct, the other wrong. Underline the correct word:
   a) William can (ran, run) faster than (I, me).
   b) It was (me, I) who (did, done) it.
   c) George and (he, him) (has, have) gone on holiday.
   d) Between you and (me, I) I think they (was, were) wrong.
   e) (He, Him) and (me, I) are twelve years of age.

2. A number of sheep is called a **flock**. Insert the most suitable word in each of the following:
   a) a _____ of wolves
   b) a _____ of bees
   c) a _____ of herring
   d) a _____ of cattle
   e) a _____ of ships
   f) a _____ of singers
   g) a _____ of thieves

3. In the following sentences underline the correct word of the two words within brackets:
   a) You ought to visit her now (but, that) you know where she stays.
   b) Write down the answers (as, when) you were taught.
   c) The boy tried hard (but, that) he failed.
   d) (Than, When) he comes let us know.
   e) The man was careful (except, lest) he should fall.

4. a) Give the plural of:
      deer, mouse, lily, tooth, woman.
   b) Give the masculine of:
      cow, duchess, duck, actress, niece.

5. By accident the sentences of this story were jumbled. Rearrange them in their proper order:
   Fortunately he saved her from serious injury.
   Suddenly her ball rolled into the middle of the road, and she ran after it.
   A passer-by saw the girl's danger and ran to her aid.
   A little girl was playing on a busy street.
   At that moment a car came dashing round the corner.

Test 14

1. In the following sentences underline the correct word of the two words within brackets:
   a) How he managed it remains a (duty, mystery).
   b) James was honest and (deceptive, diligent).
   c) The stranger asked if I could (direct, inform) him to the station.

d) The (remedy, illness) or cure is very simple.

e) His opinion differed (against, from) mine.

2. a) Punctuate the following correctly:

   tell me said the old gentleman what is your name.

   b) Form adjectives from:

   reason, success, south, fool, France.

3. Use the correct prepositions in the blank spaces:
   a) The bottle was filled _____ water.
   b) He was told not to meddle _____ the toys.
   c) The two brothers divided the apple _____ them.
   d) That hat is similar _____ mine.
   e) I hope I can rely _____ you.

4. With whom do you associate the following?
   Example: anvil – blacksmith

   a) rifle _____
   b) prescription _____
   c) telescope _____
   d) spectacles _____
   e) letters _____
   f) pulpit _____
   g) sheep _____
   h) joy-stick _____

5. Opposite each phrase are groups of words in brackets. Underline the group of words in brackets which gives the correct meaning of the phrase:

   down in the mouth (speaking quickly) (in low spirits)

   a peppery individual (a quick-tempered person) (a happy person)

   out of sorts (not well) (of great courage)

   hard up (good enough) (short of money)

   beside oneself (annoyed and angry) (nothing to do)

Test 15

1. a) Underline the correct word of the words in brackets:

   A man who writes stories is an (artist, author, sculptor).

   A bed on board ship is called a (bunk, cabin, saloon).

   A person who hoards money is a (martyr, miser, cashier).

   A vessel for holding flowers is a (caddy, scuttle, vase).

   The flesh of a cow is called (beef, mutton, pork).

   b) Underline the group of words in brackets which gives the correct meaning of the phrase:

   to play the game (to act fairly) (to run quickly)

   to bury the hatchet (to chop wood) (to make peace)

   to cut a dash (to hurt one's leg) (to be very showy)

to smell a rat (to be suspicious) (to hunt mice)

to show the white feather (to be cowardly) (to be proud of an achievement)

2. Underline the correct word of the two words in brackets:

a) Bernice as well as George (was, were) at the circus.

All of you but Tom (has, have) the wrong answer.

A purse containing three coins (was, were) found.

One and all (is, are) going to the concert.

Neither the one nor the other (is, are) right.

b) His friend and (he, him) travelled to Paris.

Was it (I, me) you saw there?

Between you and (I, me) I am sure he is wrong.

Emily is younger than (I, me).

Let you and (I, me) hide.

3. a) Willie has (grew, grown) very tall.

The town crier (rang, rung) his bell.

The boy (began, begun) to look for his pencil.

Has he (wrote, written) to his cousin?

The lion (sprung, sprang) at the timid deer.

b) The girl wept (bitterly, faintly).

The boy fell (clearly, heavily).

The man crept (harshly, stealthily).

The lady waited (patiently, deeply).

My friend sprang (quickly, plainly).

4. a) He neither reads (or, nor) writes well.

(Now, When) we arrived we searched for our luggage.

Charles is stronger (as, than) I am.

I know (that, before) Tom is a good scholar.

I could not pay him (that, for) I had no money.

b) The hunter went in pursuit (to, of) the animal.

He suffers (from, of) a swollen head.

I was sorry to part (of, with) that picture.

The girl complained (with, of) a sore foot.

The man disagreed (of, with) him.

5. a) In the following lists of words, one word in each list is out of place.
Underline this word.

copper, lead, tin, earth, silver

rain, cold, snow, sleet, hail

corn, rye, barley, wheat, raisins

ear, nose, mouth, knee, chin

linen, leather, silk, cotton, wool

b) Underline the word of the same kind as the first three words in each line:

river, brook, stream (mountain, tributary, island)

sofa, chair, stool (cupboard, wardrobe, couch)

limestone, marble, slate (granite, cement, mortar)

sword, dagger, spear (revolver, rifle, lance)

kitten, puppy, calf (duck, lamb, horse)

6. Underline the correct word of the two words in brackets:

a) The ship tied up at the (key, quay).

He was not (allowed, aloud) to go.

The jacket was made of (course, coarse) cloth.

The (pail, pale) moon rose above the hills.

We picked up shells on the (beach, beech).

b) Rearrange the following sentences in their proper order so that they form a short story:

This he did to the great joy of the onlookers.

He refused to bow to the Governor's hat.

He ordered him to shoot an apple from his son's head.

The Governor wished to punish him for his disobedience.

William Tell was a famous archer in Switzerland.

Test 16

1. Underline the correct word of the group of words in brackets:

a) A person who eats too much is a (miser, glutton, hypocrite).

b) A woman who sells vegetables is a (greengrocer, florist, vegetarian).

c) John, who is my aunt's son, is my (nephew, brother, cousin).

d) A soldier who rides on horseback is in the (marines, cavalry, infantry).

e) A wooden shelter made for a dog is a (byre, stable, kennel).

2. Give words opposite in meaning to:

present	_____	bitter	_____
entrance	_____	polite	_____
east	_____	danger	_____
guilty	_____	lost	_____

3. Underline the correct word in each of the brackets:

(Who, Whom) do you think I (saw, seen)?

All but one (was, were) saved when the ship (sank, sunk).

Each of the men (has, have) a right to (their, his) opinion.

Between you and (I, me), the girls (wasn't, weren't) pleased.

Let Maria and (me, I) stay after the others have (gone, went).

4. We say "as black as coal". Supply the missing words in the following:

as blind as _____   as cold as _____

as quiet as _____   as good as _____

as gentle as _____   as sharp as _____

as happy as _____   as fresh as _____

5. Following are five sentences, which, if arranged properly, would make a short story. Rearrange them in proper order:

The bird, highly flattered, opened her mouth to sing.

One day a crow spied a piece of cheese on a window sill.

The cheese fell and was soon eaten by the crafty animal.

She picked it up and flew to a neighbouring tree.

A cunning fox approached and praised her voice.

Test 17

1. Christmas Day comes in the month of _____.

Snapper, herring, salmon, bass are all _____.

The masculine of **aunt** is _____.

_____ is the feminine of **hero**.

State the plural of **tooth**.

A number of **sheep** is called a _____.

We say "as **sharp** as a _____".

A person who works on an **anvil** is a _____.

What animal **brays**?

The word for a **young hen** is _____.

2. Give words opposite in meaning to:

defend, stranger, reveal, throw, compliment.

3. The noun formed from **select** is _____.

_____ is the adjective formed from **attract**.

Give a verb corresponding to **broad**.

Form an adverb from **joy**.

Give a compound word with **grand** as part of it.

4. **Bird** is to **air** as **fish** is to _____.

Table is to **wood** as **window** is to _____.

Food is to **hungry** as **drink** is to _____.

Nose is to **smell** as **tongue** is to _____.
Wrist is to **cuff** as **neck** is to _____.

5. In each of the following sentences underline the correct word in brackets:
Many of the pencils were (broke, broken).
Everybody (was, were) pleased with the result.
He is a little taller than (I, me).
The man could not do (nothing, anything) to help.
Neither the boy (or, nor) his sister will come.
To (who, whom) do you wish to speak?
The train moved (slow, slowly) into the station.
The food was pleasant (for, to) the taste.
We received a (strong, hearty) welcome.
Water dripped from the (brim, brink) of his hat.

6. Give words similar in meaning to:
halt, roam, margin, permit, courage.

7. Arrange the following in the correct order, beginning with **dawn**:
dusk, noon, evening, dawn, night, morning.

8. Make short sentences, one for each word, showing the correct use of the following:
their, coarse, fowl, preys, creek.

9. Give **one word** which might be used in place of the words **in bold type**:
   a) The prices were **made less than before**.
   b) The **people who were listening** applauded.
   c) The little boat **turned upside down** in the storm.
   d) The germs were **not able to be seen by the human eye**.

10. Name **ten** different **animals**.

Test 18

1. The shortest month of the year is _____.
Cassava, cauliflower, onion and pepper are all _____.
The masculine of **wife** is _____.
_____ is the feminine of **bachelor**.
State the plural of **mouse**.
A number of **thieves** is called a _____.
We say "as **bold** as _____".
A person who uses a **safety-lamp** is a _____.

What animal **neighs**?

The word for a **young fox** is _____.

2. Give words opposite in meaning to:

   arrive, sweet, fertile, legal, juvenile.

3. The noun formed from **young** is _____.

   _____ is the adjective formed from **circle**.

   Give a verb corresponding to **horror**.

   Form an adverb from **weary**.

   Give a compound word with **cup** as part of it.

4. **Walk** is to **legs** as **fly** is to _____.

   Knife is to **cut** as **gun** is to _____.

   Island is to **sea** as **lake** is to _____.

   Statue is to **sculptor** as **book** is to _____.

   Petals are to **flower** as **spokes** are to _____.

5. In each of the following sentences underline the correct word in brackets:

   A tree had (fell, fallen) across the path.

   Neither Tom nor James (is, are) at school.

   She is cleverer than (I, me).

   He should (of, have) come last night.

   Either my father (or, nor) my mother will go with me.

   I saw the lad (who, whom) won the race.

   It can be done very (easy, easily).

   He had not a penny (by, to) his name.

   She has a (healthy, spotless) character.

   I divided the sweets (between, amongst) several boys.

6. Give words similar in meaning to:

   enemy, unite, concluded, guard, envy.

7. Arrange the following in historical order:

   aeroplane, chariot, locomotive, rocket, car.

8. Make short sentences, one for each word, showing the correct use of the following:

   fourth, route, style, soled, sewing.

9. Give **one word** which might be used in place of the words **in bold type**:

   a) Smoking was **not allowed** in the garage.

   b) The motorist drove his car **slowly and carefully**.

   c) The boy **was very sorry for** his mean action.

   d) They ascended the steep steps of the **tower in which the bell was hung**.

   e) The castaways saw a ship on the **line where sea and sky seem to meet**.

10. Name **ten** different **birds**.

1. Guy Fawkes' Day is in the month of _____.
   Mosquito, beetle, moth and locust are all _____.
   The masculine of **niece** is _____.
   _____ is the feminine of **wizard**.
   State the plural of **ox**.
   A number of **pupils** is called a _____.
   We say "as **clear** as _____".
   A person who rides a **bicycle** is called a _____.
   What animal **trumpets**?
   The word for a **young goat** is _____.

2. Give words opposite in meaning to:
   ancient, purchased, private, rare, majority.

3. The noun formed from **choose** is _____.
   _____ is the adjective formed from **voice**.
   Give a verb corresponding to **deed**.
   Form an adverb from **critic**.
   Give a compound word with **ball** as part of it.

4. **Picture** is to **wall** as **carpet** is to _____.
   Graceful is to **clumsy** as **polite** is to _____.
   Descend is to **depth** as **ascend** is to _____.
   Gas is to **pipes** as **electricity** is to _____.
   Castle is to **tower** as **church** is to _____.

5. In each of the following sentences underline the correct word in brackets:
   I have never (went, gone) by bus.
   None of the pencils (is, are) missing.
   She is much older than (I, me).
   We were (learned, taught) how to read correctly.
   The boy could neither read (or, nor) write.
   (Who, Whom) do you wish to see?
   How (quick, quickly) the time has passed!
   We waited (upon, for) her at the station.
   Between you and (I, me), someone must have taken it.
   He divided the apple (between, amongst) his two brothers.

6. Give words similar in meaning to:
   vacant, remedy, concealed, grief, faith.

7. Arrange the following in historical order:
   canoe, submarine, coracle, steam-ship, sailing-ship.

8. Make short sentences, one for each word, showing the correct use of the following:
   waste, aloud, seized, medal, site.

9. Give **one word** which might be used in place of the words **in bold type**:
   a) The boy **purposely kept out of the way of** his employer.
   b) The flowers were **not real, but made of cloth, wax and paper**.
   c) The motor-car **slipped sideways across the road**.
   d) During the fire, the birds had died from **want of air to breathe**.
   e) They managed to fix it with a **sticky substance obtained from the hoofs of animals**.

10. Name **ten** different **flowers**.

Test 20

1. We live in the _____ century.
   Coal, iron, slate and lead are all _____.
   The masculine of **nun** is _____.
   _____ is the feminine of **colt**.
   State the plural of **deer**.
   A number of **singers** is called a _____.
   We say "as **keen** as _____".
   A person who uses a **palette** is an _____.
   What animal **howls**?
   The word for a **young hare** is _____.

2. Give words opposite in meaning to:
   enemy, success, expand, miser, exposed.

3. The noun formed from **receive** is _____.
   _____ is the adjective formed from **Bible**.
   Give a verb corresponding to **grass**.
   Form an adverb from **ability**.
   Give a compound word with **stone** as part of it.

4. **Sheep** is to **flock** as **tree** is to _____.
   Banana is to **peel** as **egg** is to _____.
   Speak is to **shout** as **walk** is to _____.
   When is to **time** as **where** is to _____.
   Lawyer is to **client** as **doctor** is to _____.

5. In each of the following sentences underline the correct word in brackets:

   The boy had (rose, risen) at eight o'clock.

   Every one of us (has, have) an equal chance.

   My sister is five years younger than (I, me).

   Do try (to, and) come on time.

   Neither a borrower (or, nor) a lender be.

   (Who, Whom) do you think we met?

   I managed not so (bad, badly).

   They were impatient (from, at) the delay.

   That is a (trivial, trifling) excuse.

   Let Tom and (I, me) go.

6. Give words similar in meaning to:

   commence, repair, odour, prohibited, renown.

7. Arrange the following in historical order:

   oil-lamp, firebrand, electricity, candle, gas.

8. Make short sentences, one for each word, showing the correct use of the following:

   groan, rays, rowed, cruise, cereal.

9. Give **one word** which might be used in place of the words **in bold type**:

   a) The runner was completely **tired and worn out** after the race.

   b) The injured man was **unaware of anything that was going on around him**.

   c) The rude girl continually **broke into** her parents' conversation.

   d) He **changed his appearance by dressing** himself as a native.

   e) The story caused **a state of excited feeling**.

10. Name **ten** different **fruits**.

Tests in comprehension

Test 1

Read the following passage carefully and then answer the questions below:

The story of a great river

From its source in the mountains between Sierra Leone and Guinea to its delta in Eastern Nigeria the mighty Niger will have travelled some 4,000 kilometres. This nine-month-long journey to the far-off Gulf of Guinea will take it through many countries and some of the most varied scenery in the world.

From the high mountains in the Fouta Djallon region through the dense forests of Guinea it flows, gaining in size from its many tributaries. Its waters create the fertile plains of the Republic of Mali before reaching the desert regions beyond Timbuktu whence it turns south-eastwards to flow between the republics of Niger and Benin.

It is here that it enters Nigeria, that great African state and, more than half its journey over, is put to work. Vast hydro-electric plants provide for the needs of Nigeria's millions and for the industry of this huge country. Here, too, irrigation schemes, fed by its waters, assist in food production and its use, with specially designed vessels, to facilitate travel, trade and the transport of goods. And everywhere there are fishermen casting their nets.

At Lokoja, where the Niger is joined by its greatest tributary, the Benue, it turns sharply southwards to flow majestically past Onitsha and presently to form its vast delta. This delta, hot and humid, is a place of great rainforests, mangrove swamps and a network of waterways taking the Niger at last to the sea. Here, too, and in the sea offshore, are the oil-fields which make Nigeria one of the main oil producers of the Commonwealth of Nations.

1. Where is the source of the Niger? (1)
2. Name three towns on its banks. (2)
3. Through which countries does it pass? (1)
4. In which country is its delta? (1)
5. In your own words describe a delta. (3)
6. In your own words describe a mangrove. (2)
7. What is opposite in direction to south-east? (2)
8. What confluence occurs at Lokoja? (2)
9. Find out and write about Mungo Park. (5)
10. Write short notes on the following:
    Hausa, Yoruba, Ibo, Fulani, Tiv, Kanuri. (6)

Total 25

Test 2

Read the following passage carefully and then answer the questions below:

Homework interrupted

Tabu looked up from his book, in a lazy way at first, to see what had made the noise. Then he went stiff with fright. At an arm's length away from his chair, something moved. A shape glided smoothly along the window frame. He saw a flat head held up by a slender neck. A puff adder!

The snake stopped and lay without moving. It looked dead. But all the time it was trying to sense if any food was in the room.

Tabu felt trapped in his chair, yet he knew he must warn his sister. He thought of what his father had told him so often. He wanted to whisper, but his mouth and tongue were dry with shock. He dared not move. His throat clicked as he tried to utter some sound. If only she would look at him!

Masya must have felt that there was something strange about his silence, for she turned her head to glance at him. When she saw the fear on his face, she swiftly shifted round, looking at his glazed eyes. She moved her head to see what those eyes were fixed on, then covered her mouth to stifle her gasp of terror.

(From *World Wide Adventure Series* Reader 5 – published by Robert Gibson.)

1. What had the snake come for? (1)
2. Why would it stop and lie without moving? (1)
3. What made Tabu feel trapped in his chair? (2)
4. What effects did Tabu's fear have on him? (2)
5. Why would he wish to warn his sister? (2)
6. What do you think Tabu's father had told him so often? (2)
7. What caused Masya to look at Tabu? (1)
8. How did she come to see where the danger was? (1)
9. Why did she cover her mouth? (2)
10. What might have happened if Tabu had moved? (2)
11. What do you think Tabu wanted to warn his sister to do or not to do? (4)
12. What would you have done in Tabu's place? (5)

Total 25

Test 3

Read the following passage carefully and then answer the questions below:

The fox

The fox is probably the most intelligent of all quadrupeds. It is allied to the dog and closely resembles the Alsatian, the wolf, the hyena, the coyote (prairie-wolf of North America), the dingo (native dog of Australia), and the dhole (wild dog of India). Its chief points of difference from the others are the sharper muzzle and the shorter legs in proportion to the size of the body. Its tail or "brush" is also longer, and its ears more erect.

The fox has eyes with pupils that contract in strong light and expand in darkness. This enables the animal to hunt at night. It excavates its own lair by burrowing much like a rabbit, but frequently it is a thief in this respect as it steals burrows from other animals and converts them into its own "earth". The cunning and slyness of the animal is shown by the number of exits to its lair. As many as ten bolt-holes from the fox's "earth" have been counted. Its power of scent is very acute, and its hearing very highly developed. The animal has a peculiar strong scent, which leaves the "trail" in the so-called sport of fox-hunting. When the chase is keen, Reynard frequently escapes by dashing into wide and open drainpipes. For this reason one may see gratings placed over the mouths of many roadside and field drains. When cornered by the hounds the animal has been known to climb roofs of houses and to dash into nearby cottages in desperate efforts to shake off its pursuers.

1. What is a quadruped? (1)
2. Name ten animals mentioned in the passage. (5)
3. Give four points of difference between the fox and the dog. (4)
4. Why is the fox able to hunt at night? (1)
5. Name any other creature which hunts at night. (1)
6. What two words are used for the fox's den? (2)
7. Of what use are bolt-holes? (1)
8. What animal does the fox resemble when digging? (1)
9. Give two reasons why the fox is a difficult animal to catch. (2)
10. What enables the hounds to track down the fox? (1)
11. What special name is sometimes given to a fox? (1)
12. According to the passage, why do gratings sometimes cover drainpipes? (1)
13. What is meant by "When the chase is keen"? (1)
14. Give the meanings of the following words as used in the passage:
    contract, excavates, frequently, converts, scent, peculiar. (3)

Total 25

Test 4

Read the following passage (supposed to have been written by a boy) and then answer the questions below:

When I had finished breakfast the squire gave me a note addressed to John Silver, at the sign of the Spy-glass, and told me I should easily find the place by following the line of the docks, and keeping a bright look-out for a little tavern with a large brass telescope for sign. I set off, overjoyed at this opportunity to see some more of the ships and seamen, and picked my way among a great crowd of people and carts and bales, for the dock was now at its busiest, until I found the tavern in question. It was a bright enough little place of entertainment. The sign was newly painted; the windows had neat red curtains; the floor was newly sanded. There was a street on either side, and an open door on

both, which made the large, low room pretty clear to see in, in spite of clouds of tobacco smoke. The customers were mostly sea-faring men; and they talked so loudly that I hung at the door, almost afraid to enter. As I was waiting, a man came out of a side room, and, at a glance, I was sure he must be Long John. His left leg was cut off close by the hip, and under the left shoulder he carried a crutch, which he managed with wonderful dexterity. He seemed in the most cheerful spirits, whistling as he moved about among the tables.

1. To whom was the squire's note addressed? (1)
2. Where was this person to be found? (1)
3. At what time of day did the boy set out? (1)
4. What route was he to take? (1)
5. Why was the boy overjoyed? (2)
6. When the boy had found the tavern in question, what did he notice about
    a) the sign, b) the windows, c) the floor? (3)
7. Who were the customers? (1)
8. Why was the boy almost afraid to enter? (2)
9. Where was John Silver when the boy first looked into the tavern? (1)
10. What nickname is used in the passage? (2)
11. Describe John Silver's unusual appearance. (4)
12. How do you know Silver was happy? (1)
13. Give another word of the same meaning for each of the following:
    spy-glass, tavern, opportunity, glance, dexterity. (5)

Total 25

Test 5

Read the following passage carefully and then answer the questions below:

Sightseeing in Singapore

You do not have to go far in Singapore to discover the unexpected or the unusual. A stroll through Chinatown could bring you face to face with a cartful of masks for people to wear to represent mythical or historical characters in a procession or an operatic or theatrical performance during some festival – heads of heroes and villains, horses and lions, unicorns and dragons, all crafted with loving care and selling at surprisingly low prices. Go and listen to the early morning "concert" of birdsong from hundreds of caged birds. Have your initials carved in semi-precious stone to make your own personal seal. Notice the old women working on a construction site, clad in black and wearing red head-dresses. These are the Samsui sisters who have voluntarily chosen to adopt this way of life and remain unmarried.

The variety of things to do in Singapore is endless. Relax on a tropical beach, take a stroll through a lush green park or visit an Indian temple. You can spend hours in the Zoological Gardens with their world-famous Orang-utan colony, spot 350 different species among the 7,000 birds in the Bird Park, see the Orchid Garden with its thousands of blooms that would cost a king's ransom in London, or visit a crocodile farm.

After your sightseeing you may be hungry, and there is no better place to be hungry than in Singapore. Rich aromas will draw you to one of Singapore's 8,000 open-air food-stalls offering Chinese, Malay, and Indian dishes in all their infinite variety – with a banana leaf, perhaps, to serve as your plate and end the day with yet another surprise.

(*Information Source:* Singapore Tourist Promotion Board.)

1. What is a *mythical* character? (2)
2. How is a *historical* character different? (2)
3. How do *operatic* and *theatrical* productions differ? (2)
4. What does *crafted* mean? Why is it a good word here? (2)
5. Why would the low prices be surprising? (2)
6. Why is the word "concert" in inverted commas? (2)
7. What would be the purpose of having a personal seal? (2)
8. What is a construction site? (2)
9. What does the word *species* mean? What is its singular? (2)
10. What does *a king's ransom* mean and why? (2)
11. What would be the purpose of a crocodile farm? (2)
12. Distinguish *flavours, aromas, smells* and *perfumes*. (3)

Total 25

Test 6

Read the following passage carefully and then answer the questions below:

The long trek

Steve reckoned that they were about three miles from the river, if there was still a river. By now, it might be just a trickle of slow-moving water, or a bed of dried mud, full of tumbleweed and stones.

He closed his eyes to slits as he peered through the clouds of dust – red dust kicked up by hundreds of hoofs. The cattle that streamed past him as he sat slumped in his saddle were as tired and worn out as the exhausted men who drove them.

Some of them bellowed with fear and pain. The calves pushed their noses into the sides of the cows that had no more milk to feed them. All of them were mad with thirst and very thin. From their knob-like backbones, the drawn skin was tight over the fleshless haunches. Their ribs curved like the bars of a cage over their sunken flanks. They were starving.

They had trekked from the cattle stations in the north of Australia where usually heavy rains filled streams and pools. But this was a year of drought. The burning sun, which had sucked up the last drops of water, had left the ground cracked and dry. Wide, dangerous ruts had formed in the earth. They were deep and broad enough to wedge a man's boot when he walked. There was only one thing to do. The cattle must be driven many miles south, to the river; or they would die.

(From *World Wide Adventure Series* Reader 5 – published by Robert Gibson.)

1. Why did Steve sit "slumped" in his saddle? (2)
2. What did he fear might have happened to the river? (3)
3. Why were the animals' backbones like knobs? (1)
4. What other effects had the drought had on them? (3)
5. What is a drought? (1)
6. Why would the ground have cracks? (2)
7. Had the sun really "sucked" up drops of water? (3)
8. Why were the ruts in the earth dangerous? (1)
9. If the river was dry, what then? (4)
10. What effects would a drought have in your area? (5)

Total 25

Test 7

Read the following passage carefully and then answer the questions below:

The death of James I of Scotland

The king, while he was staying at Perth, took up his residence in the abbey of Black Friars, there being no convenient palace in the town, and this made it easier for his enemies to carry out their purpose, as his guards and officers were staying in different houses.

Just as James, having dismissed all his attendants, was preparing to go to bed, the Highland woman who had already warned him at the ferry, again demanded permission to speak with the king, but was refused on account of the lateness of the hour. Suddenly a clashing of armour was heard in the garden and flashes of light from torches were thrown against the windows. The king, hearing the voice of Sir Robert Graham, his deadly enemy, guessed that the intruders had come to murder him. He called to the ladies to keep the door as well as they could, while he tried to get out at the windows, but the bars would not budge. By the help of tongs, however, he lifted a plank of the flooring, and let himself down into a narrow vault beneath. This vault had formerly had an opening into the courtyard of the convent, by which he might have made his escape, but the unfortunate James forgot that, only three days before, he had caused the opening to be built up, because when he played at ball in the courtyard the ball used to roll into the vault through that hole.

The queen and her women endeavoured as well as they might to keep the door shut, and one of them, Katherine Douglas, boldly thrust her arm across the door in place of the bar, which the conspirators had removed the day before.

1. Why did the king stay in an abbey at Perth? (1)
2. Why did the king's enemies find it easy to attack him in the abbey? (1)
3. Why did the woman want to speak with the king? (2)
4. Why was the Highland woman turned from the door? (1)
5. What two things alarmed the king and the ladies? (2)
6. Why did the king fear the intruders? (2)
7. Why could James not jump from a window? (1)
8. How did the king escape from the room? (1)
9. When the king let himself into the vault what did he expect to do? (2)
10. Why had the vault entrance been closed? (2)
11. How had the conspirators prepared, the day before, for the murder? (2)
12. Describe a "torch" of the time of this story. (2)
13. Give another word with the same meaning for each of the following:
    residence, convenient, budge, unfortunate, endeavoured, conspirators. (6)

Total 25

Test 8

Read this passage carefully and then answer the questions below:

Shipwreck on a coral island

A huge wave snatched up the oar that we had decided to cling to instead of joining the ship's crowded boat, and ...

I came to on the shore to find young Peterkin trying to staunch the flow of blood from my badly cut brow, and learned from Jack that we appeared to be the only survivors, alone on an uninhabited island.

It soon occurred to Peterkin, the youngest of us at fourteen, that hunger and thirst might be a problem. The ship's stores were sunk in deep water. What would we do? Jack pointed up to the branched head of a coconut palm. "There, look!" he said. "Nuts at all stages."

In no time Peterkin had monkeyed up and tossed down three nuts about the size of a football.

"Let's visit the wreck first," said Jack, "and then eat."

Though only eighteen himself, Jack was our natural leader and no one objected, Peterkin comforting himself by telling us that he'd rather find a spring, and have a drink, than eat.

"Then hop up that tree again," said Jack, "and throw down another nut, a green one this time, unripe."

Surprised, but always game, Peterkin did as he was told.

"Now cut a hole in it with your knife and clap it to your mouth."

Peterkin did as directed, and we both burst into uncontrolled laughter at the changes that instantly passed over his face. No sooner had he put the nut to his mouth and thrown back his head to catch what came out, than his eyes opened to twice their ordinary size, while his throat moved vigorously in the act of swallowing. Then a look of intense delight spread over his face except, of course, his mouth, which was otherwise engaged. At length he stopped, drew a long breath, and exclaimed, "Nectar! Perfect nectar!"

(Adapted from *The Coral Island* by R. M. Ballantyne.)

1. What happened between the first and second paragraphs? (2)
2. How are we expected to know this? (2)
3. Why is *staunch* a better word than *stop* (paragraph 2)? (2)
4. What did Jack mean by "nuts at all stages"? (2)
5. What do the words *monkeyed* and *hop* suggest? (2)
6. Why could they not get food from the wreck? (2)
7. Why did Jack first speak of eating but not drinking? (2)
8. Which sentences show Jack as a good leader? (2)
9. Is *objecting* different from *refusing*? (2)
10. Why did the others laugh at Peterkin? (2)
11. What feelings can make us wide-eyed? (2)
12. What does "otherwise engaged" mean? (1)
13. What was the point of exclaiming "Nectar!"? (2)

Total 25

Test 9

Read this passage carefully and then answer the questions below:

Nature and the traveller in the Caribbean

Nature shows off to the traveller in the Caribbean. Start in the Cayman Islands and she introduces you to some of her prize travellers, the turtles that swim thousands of miles to these sandy shores to lay their eggs.

Watch Neptune's gliders, the "flying" fish, skimming the tips of waves as you make for Jamaica and sail into one of the world's great natural harbours. Go ashore and see huge crawling monsters clawing out mountains of bauxite from which will come aluminium, "silver from clay", to be made into kitchen utensils and tomorrow's jumbo jets.

Don't miss seeing the phenomenal lush growth of a tropical rainforest, on Dominica, where the tree canopy blots out the sun.

On Barbados stand and watch the Atlantic's majestic rollers crashing against the foot of the island's northern rock-face, tossing up spray twice the height of the cliffs. There too you will marvel, as elsewhere, at the unimaginable number of tiny coral insects that had to live and die to form these miles of bright clean sands, reefs and whole coral islands.

Drive over the wild moon landscape of the crater of St Lucia's Soufrière volcano, its deafening jets of steam showing it is not yet dead, only sleeping. Then take your pictures, as everyone does, of the island's twin sugar-loaf mountains rising 800 metres sheer out of the sea, and move on, perhaps flying over the volcanoes of St Vincent and Grenada, their craters now occupied by lakes, to busy Trinidad. Here see the pitch lake Sir Walter Raleigh used to waterproof his ships' hulls, and which today, after four hundred years, still supplies asphalt for our roads.

And these ships in the bay? Nature will fill them again and again with the oil she has made from the remains of living things that lived here long before history.

Now step over to South America and see one final marvel, Guyana's Kaieteur Falls, five times the height of Niagara, a spectacular end to an unforgettable trip.

1. Does nature "show off"? What is meant? (2)
2. In what way are the turtles "prize travellers"? (2)
3. Does the writer think flying fish really fly? (2)
4. What "crawling monster" would you see in Jamaica? (2)
5. Why is aluminium called "silver from clay"? (2)
6. What makes the forests on Dominica so lush? (2)
7. Compare *rollers* with other words that could be used. (2)
8. How are coral reefs formed? (2)
9. What do the words *moon landscape* suggest? (2)
10. Is it better to call the volcano *sleeping* than *dormant*? (2)
11. Explain the second last paragraph. (3)
12. What makes things *spectacular*? (2)

Total 25

Test 10

Read this passage carefully and then answer the questions below:

Monday morning

Monday morning found Tom Sawyer miserable. Monday morning always found him so, because it began another week's slow suffering in school. He generally began that day with wishing he had had no intervening holiday; it made the going into captivity and fetters again so much more odious.

Tom lay thinking. Presently it occurred to him that he wished he was sick; then he could stay at home from school. Here was a vague possibility. He canvassed his system. No ailment was found, and he investigated again. This time he thought he could detect colicky symptoms, and he began to encourage them with considerable hope. But they soon grew feeble and presently died wholly away. He reflected further. Suddenly he discovered something. One of his upper teeth was loose. This was lucky; he was about to groan, as a "starter", as he called it, when it occurred to him that if he came into court with that argument his aunt would pull it out, and that would hurt. So he thought he would hold the tooth in reserve for the present, and seek further. Nothing offered for some little time, and then he remembered hearing the doctor tell about a certain thing that laid up a patient for two or three weeks and threatened to make him lose a finger. So the boy eagerly drew his sore toe from under the sheet and held it up for inspection. But now he did not know the necessary symptoms. However, it seemed well worthwhile to chance it, so he fell to groaning with considerable spirit.

Mark Twain

1. Where was Tom when he was doing his thinking? (1)
2. What prospect was making him miserable? (1)
3. What made the misery worse on Mondays? (1)
4. What was the purpose of his thinking? (1)
5. What three ideas did he have for achieving his purpose? (3)
6. What caused him to reject his first idea? (1)
7. How do we know he thought the second idea was better? (1)
8. Why did he not adopt this second idea? (1)
9. How did he set about carrying out his third plan? (1)
10. What weakness can you see in this third plan? (1)
11. In what sense was Tom facing captivity and fetters? (1)
12. What is meant by the words "canvass" (compare "canvas") and "system"? (2)
13. What would Tom do in "canvassing his system"? (2)
14. In the phrase "came into court with that argument" what court is meant, and what argument? (2)
15. What is meant by holding the tooth "in reserve"? (1)
16. What is the difference between a symptom and an ailment? (2)
17. Which words used in the passage refer to *feelings*, and which other words refer to *thinking*? (3)

Total 25

Test II

Read this passage carefully and then answer the questions which follow:

Africa is the second largest continent and is a land of great contrasts. It has burning deserts and luxurious forests teeming with animal life.

North of the Sahara Desert on the Mediterranean coast are the Arab States, to the South are the ex-colonies, now self-governing. Europe is only 9 miles from the North African coast at the Straits of Gibraltar. To the North East, in Egypt, the Suez Isthmus joins Africa to Asia. The Isthmus is cut by the 72-mile stretch of the Suez Canal which provides passage for ships from the Indian Ocean to the Mediterranean Sea and the Atlantic Ocean.

The equator passes through the centre of Africa at Mount Kenya, and most of the continent lies in the tropics, i.e. between the tropic of Cancer and the tropic of Capricorn.

Because of Africa's smooth coastline there are few inlets and bays.

The largest island is the Republic of Madagascar in the Indian Ocean. The Cape Verde Islands, the Canaries, and Madeira are all groups of islands off the North West coast.

Most of the land is one vast plateau. There is only a narrow coastal plain in most places but this broadens in the North East and North West. The plateau is stepped, and on each "step" there are wide, flat tracts of land with few mountains.

One remarkable feature of the geography of the continent, and indeed of the world, is the Great Rift Valley, formed where the land has sunk between two faults in the Earth's crust. One branch of this rift is occupied by Lake Albert, Lake Tanganyika, Lake Nyasa and the last 200 miles of the course of the Zambesi River. The other branch runs through Kenya from Lake Nyasa and is occupied by the Red Sea in the North, continuing up the Gulf of Aqaba and the valley of the River Jordan in Asia.

There are three great deserts which form two fifths of the continental area, the Sahara in the North (the largest in area) the Kalahari in the South and the Namib along the South West coast.

The highest mountain is Kilimanjaro, with its 19,340 feet (5895 metre) Uhuru Peak, which is always snow-covered though almost on the equator. This and other mountains are volcanic in origin and a few volcanoes are still active. The Atlas mountains cut off the Sahara from the western Mediterranean and the Atlantic. The second largest fresh-water lake in the world, Lake Victoria, lies between the two arms of the Rift Valley.

Africa's rivers include some of the longest in the world. The Nile drains huge areas from the equator to the Mediterranean, providing Egypt with rich silt for crops and water to irrigate them. The Congo Basin is one of the world's great tropical rainforests. The Niger probably waters more countries than any other river. The Zambesi boasts the world's greatest waterfalls and, like the Volta, has been put to work to provide millions with electricity.

1. The passage is about:
    A. *the Sahara Desert*   B. *the geography of Africa*
    C. *the African coastline*   D. *the tropic of Capricorn.*

2. Which of these has nothing to do with the passage?
    A. *Madagascar*   B. *drilling for oil*
    C. *the Sahara Desert*   D. *the Indian Ocean.*

3. From the passage we learn:
    A. *Africa is the second largest continent.*
    B. *Africa is a winter resort of migrant birds.*
    C. *Africa is moving slowly (drifting).*
    D. *Africa has four deserts.*

4. According to the passage, Africa is:
    A. *one vast plateau*   B. *full of active volcanoes*
    C. *surrounded by islands*   D. *made up of jungle.*

5. The Atlas mountains:
    A. *lie beside the Mediterranean*   B. *meet the Indian Ocean*
    C. *join Egypt at the Suez Canal*   D. *cut off the Sahara from the western Mediterranean.*

6. From the passage we can conclude:
    A. *Africa has a rocky coastline.*
    B. *Africa is surrounded on three sides by oceans.*
    C. *it is possible to sail right round Africa.*
    D. *snow is unknown in Kenya.*

7. The largest island, or group of islands, off the African coast is:
    A. *Madeira*   B. *Canaries*
    C. *the Cape Verde Islands*   D. *Madagascar.*

8. There is a narrow coastal plain:
    A. *to the North around the Atlas mountains*
    B. *south of the Equator*
    C. *to the South West at the Namib Desert*
    D. *in most places.*

9. From the passage we learn that the Great Rift Valley was formed by:
    A. *erosion due to weather*
    B. *volcanic eruptions*
    C. *sinking of the land between cracks in the Earth's crust*
    D. *rivers gouging out a channel for themselves.*

10. From the passage, which of these is not a feature of African geography?
   A. *the Kalahari Desert*
   B. *ships in the Suez Canal*
   C. *the smooth coastline*
   D. *the great plateau*

11. Where does the Mediterranean meet the Atlantic?
   A. *at Madagascar*
   B. *at Lake Victoria*
   C. *at the Strait of Gibraltar*
   D. *near the Sahara Desert*

Standard English pronunciation

Unless you pronounce your words correctly giving the vowels and consonants their correct value, the sounds which you make will not be understood. In this chapter we set out most of the variety of sounds used in speaking English, give you practice in these sounds and identify, and help you to avoid, the common errors of speech. Throughout this chapter, where further practice is considered desirable, reference has been made to the lists of words in *Sounds of Words* Books 1 or 2 (published by Hodder Gibson).

We will start with the simple single vowel sounds and proceed by easy stages to cover and give practice in all the necessary sounds. Remember to practise the starters until you sound perfect before going on to complete words.

Some *a* sounds

Practise starters *ma'*, *pa'*, *ra'*, *ca'*, *fa'*.

ma'n, pa'n, ra'n, ca'n, fa'n, Dan, Sam, Pam, tan, yam

(For further practice SOW Book 1, pages 7 & 8.)

Some *e* sounds

Practise starters *be'*, *le'*, *ke'*, *pe'*, *te'*.

be'g, le'g, ke'g, pe'g, Te'd, bed, led, fed, sell, fell

(For further practice SOW Book 1, pages 11 & 12.)

Some *i* sounds

Practise starters *wi'*, *ki'*, *i'*, *bi'*.

wi'll, wi'n, ki'd, li'd, bi'll, lip, sip, pick, sick, wick

(For further practice SOW Book 1, pages 15 & 16.)

Some *o* sounds

Practise starters *fo'*, *no'*, *lo'*, *so'*.

fo'g, no'd, lo'g, no't, so'p, bog, cot, dog, for, got

(For further practice SOW Book 1, page 19.)

Some *u* sounds

Practise starters *gu'*, *bu'*, *cu'*, *du'*.

gu'n, gu'm, bu'n, cu't, du'll, bus, cup, fur, hurt, just

(For further practice SOW Book 1, pages 21 & 22.)

Revision

it, pat, pig, us, van, mat, jug, bed, lad, met, mutt, tan, led, yam, cup, dog,
Meg, hog, hug, sip
For further revision in the sounds you have just learned, turn to SOW
Book 1, page 23.

ck

Remember to prolong the vowel and emphasise the final *ck*.
Practise starters *ba'*, *ne'*, *ti'*, *to'*, *su'*.
ba'ck, ne'ck, ti'ck, to'ck, su'ck, lack, peck, sick, lock, luck
(For further practice SOW Book 1, page 25.)

Emphasise the final consonants

damp, send, kept, pack, rust, went, sand, text, rack, pump
(For further practice SOW Book 1, pages 27, 28, 29, 30.)

Get the "starters" correct

bla'ck, cri'sp, sti'ck, tra'mp, sta'ck, dre'ss, dru'm, lucky, sorry, fuzzy
(For further practice SOW Book 1, pages 32, 33, 35.)

The missing e

The final *e* is not pronounced in certain words.
candle, dazzle, paddle, fizzle, battle, cattle, kettle, puddle
(For further practice SOW Book 1, page 39.)

The *sh* sound

Practise the *sh* "starters" *sha'*, *she'*, *shi'*, *sho'*, *shu'*.
shirt, shop, sham, shell, shed, shut, shock, shot, short, shod
(For further practice SOW Book 1, page 41.)
Note that *sh* at the end of the words has the same sound.
fish, dish, crush, crash
(For further practice SOW Book 1, page 42.)

The *th* sounds

Practise the *th* starters and endings.
thumb, cloth, wrath, lath, that, thong, thing, them, bath
(For further practice SOW Book 1, pages 43 & 44.)

The *ch* sound

Practise the starters and endings.
chick, church, match, branch, latch, batch, chap, chip, check
(For further practice SOW Book 1, pages 45 & 46.)

The *wh* sound

Practise the starters *whi'*, *wha'*, *whe'*.
whi'p, whi'sk, whi'stle, wha't, when, where, whit, whack, whiz, whim
(For further practice SOW Book 1, pages 47 & 48.)

The *ng* sound

wing, bang, sting, hang, sang, rang, long, rung
(For further practice SOW Book 1, page 50.)

a – e

The silent *e* changes the *a* sound.
The silent *e* makes *a* as in *man*, sound *ā* as in *day*, *hay*, *lay*.
ba'ke, ba'se, ha're, ta'ble, case, lake, make, cake
(For further practice SOW Book 2, pages 4 & 5.)

i – e

The silent *e* changes the *i* sound.
The silent *e* changes the *i* as in *lip*, *pip* to *i* as in *fire*.
Practise starters *fi'*, *mi'*, *pi'*, *li'*, *hi'*.
fire, mine, pipe, like, hide, dice, white
(For further practice SOW Book 2, pages 6 & 7.)

o – e

The silent e changes the o sound as in *rod* to the o as in *rode*.
nose, toes, roes, goes, prose, floes, notes, mote, rote
(For further practice SOW Book 2, pages 8 & 9.)

u – e

The silent e changes the u sound as in *tub, rub* to the u as in *tube*.
cube, tune, cure, use, rude, pure, glue, blue, true

y

The y sounds like *i*.
Practise the y sound – fly, sky, try, dry, fry, cry, shy, by, my.

i

Practise this new *i* sound.
tie, die, died, cried, fried, tried, spied, shied

i another sound

child, wild, mild, kind, hind, mind, blind, find, bind, rind

Revision a – e, i – e, o – e, u – e, y, i

Remember to sound your starters and go over the sounds you have just learned. Remind yourself of the various similar y and i sounds.
(For further revision SOW Book 2, pages 12 & 13.)

ay, ai

ay as in *play* and *hay* sounds the same as *ai* in *rain* and *sail*.
tray, may, say, pail, mail, day, Kay, jay, pray, wait
(For further practice SOW Book 2, pages 14 & 15.)

ee

ee as in *see, wee, wheel, week*
seek, leek, feel, heel, keep, meet, peek, reek, seek, deer, jeer, seer
(For further practice SOW Book 2, pages 16 & 17.)

ea

ea as in *ear* and *eat* sounds the same as the *ee* sound.
pea, sea, lea, dear, tear, fear, gear, hear, near, rear
(For further practice SOW Book 2, pages 18 & 19.)

qu = kw

qu as in *queen, squeak, quack.*

quads, quail, quake, quart, quench, quick, quest, quiet, quit, quiz

oo

oo as in *soot, rook, book* requires considerable practice in the starters *roo', boo', too', coo'.*
rook, pool, took, tool, hook, cook, nook
(For further practice SOW Book 2, pages 22 & 23.)

ow, ou (Two similar sounds)

ow as in *now.*
how, brown, bow, dower, power, row, sow, tower
ou as in *out.*
flour, found, shout, ouch, sound, round
(For further practice SOW Book 2, pages 24 & 25.)

wa, aw, all

wa as in *warm* is a similar sound to *aw* as in *saw:* and the *a* in *all* says *aw* as in *ball.*
wa as in *wad.*
waddle, waffle, walk, wallet, walrus, waltz, war, ward, warn, wash
aw as in *awful.*
awning, awkward, bawl, dawn, dawdle, fawn, hawk, lawn
all as in *tall.*
stall, ball, call, fall, gall, hall, mall, wall
(For further practice SOW Book 2, pages 26 & 27.)

oa

The *oa* sound is that of a long *o* as in *loaf.*
goat, goal, oak, soak, oar, oats, boat, coat, coast, foam, goal, hoax
(For further practice SOW Book 2, pages 28 & 29.)

ow

The *ow* sound, usually at the end of a word, is that of a long *o* as in *slow.*
below, arrow, sparrow, barrow, harrow, narrow, stow, row, crow, throw, lower, snow
(For further practice SOW Book 2, pages 30 & 31.)

ce = s

The *ce* sound is that of *s* as in *mice.*
lace, voice, face, choice, dice, cedar, cease, dance, lance, glance
(For further practice SOW Book 2, pages 32 & 33.)

ge = j

The *ge* sound is that of *j* as in *rage*.

cage, hinge, gem, gender, general, gentle, sage, savage, lunge, manage, strange

(For further practice SOW Book 2, page 34.)

Revision

Go back to the *ai, ay* sounds and, doing a few starters, say aloud five of each sound up to *ge*.

(Further revision SOW Book 2, page 35.)

The silent *k*

k before *n* is silent as in *knot*.

knee, knife, knock, kneel, knot, knob, know, knoll, knell

(For further practice SOW Book 2, page 36.)

The silent *w*

w before *r* is silent as in *wreck*.

wrong, wrap, write, wretch, wren, writhe, wrath, wring, wristlet, wrench, wrestle

(For further practice SOW Book 2, page 37.)

The silent *b*

lamb, thumb, dumb, numb, crumb, bomb, comb, climb

(For further practice SOW Book 2, page 38.)

The silent *t*

whistle, castle, wrestle, bustle, rustle, listen, often, soften, glisten, hustle

(For further practice SOW Book 2, page 38.)

Spelling guide

Good spelling is essential to your working life, and in all written communication. Sometimes we abbreviate spelling for text messages and other online communication, but it is important to know the original, correct spelling of all words.

Advice

- Remember the appearance of difficult words you meet in books.
- Your mind's eye is a great aid to good spelling and will often tell you what is right (or wrong).
- Consult your dictionary if in any doubt.
  Pronounce words correctly when you speak. For example:
  Pronounce the *r* after the *b* in *February*.
  Pronounce the *g* in *recognise*.
  Pronounce *secretary* as four syllables, and so on.
- Your ear will then help you to avoid many mistakes.

Though English spelling refuses to be bound by rules, some rules are worth studying for the help they can give.

i before *e*, except after *c*

The rule is only partly true, but can be improved like this:

> If sounded as *ee*, then *i* before *e*, except after *c*.
> If they sound *ay* or *eye*, then *e* before *i*.

Sounded as:	Spelling	Examples and exceptions
ee in *see*	*ie*	belief, cashier, chief, hygiene, grieve, siege
		Exceptions: protein, seize, weir, weird, and personal names like Neil, Reith, Sheila.
i in *bit*	*ie*	sieve, mischief, mischievous, handkerchief
		Exceptions: foreign, forfeit, surfeit.
ee in *see* (after *c*)	*ei*	ceiling, conceive, deceit, perceive, receipt
		Exceptions: specie, species (and see below).
ay in *day*	*ei*	eight, neighbour, reign, sovereign, weigh
ey in *eye*	*ei*	eiderdown, either, height, neither, sleight
e in *met*	*ei*	heifer, leisure
		Exceptions: friend, lieutenant.
separate	*i* + *e*	diet, glazier, soviet, science
separate	*e* + *i*	deity, homogeneity

Note: *ie* is found after *c* where *ci* sounds *sh* in:

> ancient, conscience, deficient, efficient, proficient, sufficient.

Plurals of nouns

English nouns have a great variety of plural forms – one result of inheriting and borrowing from many languages:

-s added to the singular – by far the most common form.

bats, bones, days, keys, chiefs, pianos

-es added to the singular where the singular ends in -s or another sibilant (hiss) sound, -ss, -x, -sh, -ch.

asses, lynxes, wishes, torches, lunches

-s is added to most singulars ending in -o but -es to some, and either -s or es to others.

-s for Italian, Spanish, art, musical terms, abbreviations.

pianos, altos, sopranos, sombreros, photos

-s for singulars ending in two vowels.

shampoos, studios, patios, kangaroos, videos

-es buffaloes, dominoes, mosquitoes, tomatoes, volcanoes

-s or -es flamingo(e)s, motto(e)s, stiletto(e)s

-ies replaces -y, but **not** -ay, -ey, -oy, or -uy of singulars.

allies, berries, copies, hobbies, tries, varieties

-ves replaces -f or -fe of the singular in a few words.

elves, shelves, sheaves, wives

-x is added to the singular – beaux, bureaux (from French).

-i replaces -us as in fungus, fungi; radius, radii (Latin).

-a replaces -um as in stratum, strata; datum, data (Latin).

-ices replaces -ex as in index, indices (Latin).

-es replaces -is as in axis, axes; basis, bases (Greek).

-a replaces -on as in criteria, phenomena (Greek).

See also pages 7 and 8 for plurals formed by changing a vowel, nouns with two plurals, plurals the same as singulars, nouns which have no singular, and for further examples.

Spelling words with suffixes

We add suffixes to words for a variety of purposes – for example, to make plurals, to make adjectives from nouns, adverbs from adjectives, etc. See pages 7, 91 to 96, 149 to 152.

Quite often the spelling of a base word is changed when a suffix is added. In almost every case it is the last letter of the base word that is affected.

For example:

Final *y* becomes *i*	easy+ly becomes easily.
Final *e* is dropped	hope+ing becomes hoping.
Final consonant doubled	hop+ing becomes hopping.

Final -y

Final -*y* after consonants usually becomes *i* (*ie* before *s*):

deny, denie-s, deni-ed, deni-al; luxury, luxurious;

beauty, beautiful; marry, marriage; sixty, sixtieth.

> *Exceptions:* 1. Keep the *y* before -*ing* and -*ist*:
> drying, replying, copying, copyist.
> 2. shyly, shyness, slyly, slyness, dryness, beauteous (but dryly or drily).
> 3. people's names: as in "the Kellys".

Following a vowel, final *y* is normally kept:

pay, payable, payment; prey, preys, preyed; boys, boyish; joyful, joyous; buyer, buying.

> *Exceptions:* paid, unpaid, laid, mislaid, said, slain, daily, gaily, gaiety.

Make a list of these words, close your book, and write correctly spelt new words formed from them by adding the suffix shown:

buoy, comply, defy, delay, display, flay, fry, imply, mortify, multiply, play, ply, pray, prey, pry, relay, reply, spray (+ *ed*).

ally, buoy, buy, comply, defy, obey, ply, replay, reply, vary (+ *ing*).

busy, dirty, fussy, grey, multiply, pray, pretty, silly, worry (+ *er*).

deny, duty, envy, justify, pity, play, ply, rely, vary (+ *able*).

betray, deny, try (+ *al*).

glory, joy, luxury, penury, victory (+ *ous*).

carry, marry (+ *age*).

ally, comply, dally, defy, vary (+ *ance*).

Silent -e

Keep the -*e*   before a suffix that begins with a consonant:

love, loves, lovely; hate, hateful; safe, safety.

Exceptions: argue, argument; awe, awful; due, duly; nine, ninth; true, truly; whole, wholly.

Drop the -*e*   before a suffix that begins with a vowel:

ic(e)+ed = iced; ow(e)+ing = owing;

haze, hazy; ache, aching; desire, desirous; mature, maturity.

Exceptions:

Keep the -*e*   where the base word ends in -*ce* or -*ge* **and** the suffix begins with *a* or *o*

this keeps the *c* or *g* soft before the *a* or *o*:

noticeable, manageable, courageous.

Keep the -*e*   when adding -*ing*

if the base word ends in -*ee*, -*oe* or -*ye*:

seeing, agreeing, decreeing, hoeing, shoeing, canoeing, eyeing, queueing

(but **not** in pursue, pursuing; ensue, ensuing).

Keep the -*e*   in dye, singe, tinge

this distinguishes from	dyeing dying	singeing singing.

Change the -*e*   to *i* when adding -*al*, -*ous*

to certain base words ending in -*ce*:

caprice	race	grace	vice
capricious	racial	gracious	vicious.

Make lists of these words, close your book, and write correctly spelt new words formed from them by adding the suffix shown:

agree, argue, become, die, dine, dye, judge, menace, page, pierce, pursue, queue, separate, serve, shoe, slope, sue, write (+ *ing*).

caprice, fame, grieve, nerve, outrage, prestige, space (+ *ous*).

believe, bridge, change, conceive, defence, deplore, desire, excuse, like, peace, remove, reverse, service (+ *able* or *ible*).

bare, complete, due, separate, sole, sparse, true, whole (+ *ly*).

approve, dispose, peruse, race, refuse, remove, reverse (+ *al*).

coincide, cohere, contrive, ignore, emerge, guide, resemble, revere, solve, subside, urge (+ *ance*, or + *ence*, or + *ency*).

Final consonant – when to **double** it, and when **not** to.

The *p* in *hop* is doubled, when *-ing* is added, to make *hopping*. Yet the *m* in *seem* is not doubled in the word *seeming*.

> The difference is that in *hop* the *p* has only **one** vowel in front of it, while in *seem* the *m* has **two**.

The *r* in *confer* is doubled in *conferring*, yet the *r* in *offer* is not doubled in the word *offering*.

> The difference is that, in *conferring*, the *r* is in the **stressed** syllable of the word, while in *offered* the *r* is in an unstressed syllable.

The rule that governs these differences is:

> **double** the final consonant of the base word if:
>
> 1. it is a single consonant, and
> 2. there is only a **single** vowel in front of it, and
> 3. the suffix to be added begins with a vowel, and,
> 4. (where the base word has **two** or more syllables), the final syllable of the base word is the syllable that is stressed in pronouncing the *new* word.

Examples:

Single syllable base words:

> bag, bag**g**-age; beg, beg**g**-ar; fat, fat**t**-est; red, red**d**-ish; mad**d**-en, rob**b**-ed, scrap**p**-ing; sin**n**-er, spot**t**-ed, wit**t**-y.

Longer base words (stressed syllable in bold type):

be**gin**	oc**cur**
be**ginn**-er	oc**curr**-ed
be**ginn**-ing	oc**curr**-ence
for**bid**	for**get**
for**bidd**-en	for**gett**-able
for**bidd**-ing	for**gett**-ing.

Note the effect of the position of the stress in:

con**fer**	de**fer**
con**ferr**-ing	de**ferr**-ing
confer-ence	**def**er-ent
pre**fer**	per**mitt**-ed
pre**ferr**-ing	e**licit**-ed
prefer-able	**ben**efit-ed
al**lott**ed	ac**quitt**ed
e**quipp**ing	for**gett**able
balloted	**lim**ited
galloping	**mark**etable.

Note that both **transfer*a*ble** and transfe**rri**ble are correct, and base words ending in *-our* drop the *u* before *-ous*, but not before *-able*:

glamour, glamorous; humour, humorous; honour, honourable.

Exceptions:

1. The final *-s* is not doubled in *gas-es*, but is doubled in: gass-ing, gass-ify.

2. When the suffix *-ic* is added, final consonants are not doubled: atomic, acidic, botanic, poetic, systemic.

3. A final *-c* is not doubled, but when a suffix beginning with *e* or *i* is added to the words *mimic*, *picnic*, *traffic*, the c is supplemented with a 'k' to keep the hard sound of the *c*: mimicked, picnickers, trafficking.

4. A final *w, x* or *y* is never doubled: saw-ing, tax-ation.

5. Where *-l* is the final consonant, the stress rule is ignored, and final *-l* is doubled in unstressed syllables: quarrelled, towelling, travellers, libellous, revelling.

   Exceptions: paralleled, parallelogram, scandalous, and **do not** double final *-l* before *-ise, -ism, -ist, -ity, -ize*: civil-ise, evangel-ist, formal-ity, imperial-ist, real-ism (but due**ll**ist and meda**ll**ist do double the *-l*).

6. The words *kidnap, handicap* and *worship* do not follow the stress rule either, and the final *-p* is doubled in unstressed syllables in these words: kidnapped, kidnapper; handicapped, handi-capping; worshipper, worshipping.

Say why the final consonant of the base word is not doubled in the following cases:

act-or, sail-or, bow-ing, toil-ing, loud-ness, neat-est, reveal-ed, refrain-ing, exceed-ed, instalment, derail-ed.

Make a list of these words, close your book, and write correctly spelt new words formed from them by adding the suffix shown:

develop, garden, jewel, murder, picnic, propel, traffic, scan (+ *er*).

comb, envelop, favour, parallel, quit, remit, snub, trim (+ *ed*).

envelop, expel, handicap, instal, mimic, reveal, worship (+ *ing*).

covet, danger, glamour, humour, libel, marvel, pomp, scandal (+ *ous*).

actual, civil, moral (+ *ity*).

humour, journal, medal, novel (+ *ist*).

bear, favour, honour, prefer, sever, suffer, suit, transfer (+ *able*).

Same sound – different spelling

Words

The English language includes many pairs and trios of words which sound the same but are spelt differently. See pages 73, 74 for over a hundred examples. One simply has to learn which word is spelt which way, using a dictionary if necessary.

Licence and *practice* (nouns) are often confused with *license* and *practise* (verbs), and *prophecy* (noun) with *prophesy* (verb). Remember the difference is the same as between *advice* (noun) and *advise* (verb): your ear will tell you the verbs have the *s*.

Be sure you do not confuse these spellings:

they're	short for "they are"	*it's*	short for "it is"
their	belonging to them	*its*	belonging to it (no apostrophe)
there	in that place		
you're	short for "you are"	*who's*	short for "who is"
your	belonging to you	*whose*	belonging to whom
no	the opposite of yes	*NOES*	those voting NO
know	be aware	*nose*	part of the face

Syllables

The syllables *-cede*, *-ceed* and *-sede* are often confused. It helps to remember that *supersede* is the only word with the *-sede* spelling; *exceed*, *proceed* and *succeed* are the only words with the *-ceed* spelling. All the rest – *concede*, *precede*, *recede*, etc. – have the *-cede* spelling.

Mistakes are often made with the endings *-cal* and *-cle*. The adjectives end in *-cal* and the nouns in *-cle*. Remember one of the *nouns* (names for *things*) is *article*. Some of the adjectives are: *clerical, magical, musical, physical, practical*. Some of the nouns are *article, bicycle, circle, obstacle, spectacle, vehicle*.

Similarly *principal* (ending in *-al*) is the adjective and *principle* the noun. (*Principal* is a noun when it is used of the head of a college, but it obtained this meaning only because of its adjectival sense, the Principal being the *top* member of staff).

Vowel sounds

The following list shows how a single individual vowel sound may be spelt in a dozen different ways:

Sound of	As in	Examples of other spellings of the same sound
a	bat	have, salmon
a	bath	aunt, heart, clerk, bazaar, palm, hurrah
a	bathe	nation, tail, pray, campaign, straight, bear, reins, they, reign, weigh, there, gaol, gauge, eh, dahlia
e	bet	head, said, says, leopard, leisure, any, friend, Thames, bury
e	me	theme, seen, each, field, seize, key, Caesar, police, quay, people, Beauchamp, Oedipus
i	bit	pretty, build, women, sieve, give, lyric, busy
i	idle	mine, sign, high, height, die, island, aisle, eye, try, indict, lyre, dye, choir
o	cot	shone, want, laurel, knowledge, yacht, cough
au	haul	law, tall, talk, ought, aught, broad, Vaughan
o	hero	follow, heroes, followed, furlough
o	note	both, toad, toe, dough, mow, brooch, oh, yeoman, sew, Cockburn
oo	foot	could, wolf
oo	fool	tomb, shoe, move, soup, through, truth, juice, rude, blue, sleuth, slew, manoeuvre
u	shut	blood, son, come, touch, does
u	duke	duty, due, suit, few, feud, lieu, view, impugn, ewe, you, yew
oi	coin	boy, buoy, coign
ou	loud	down, bowed, bough, McLeod
any vowel	unstressed syllables	capacity, Sarah, beaches, guinea, forfeit, terrier, hurried, tortoise, command, Europe, thoroughly, cupboard, humour, hurrah, pleasure, bury, monkey
	before an r	her, heard, bird, stirred, word, colonel, burst, blurred

Phrasal verbs

Component parts

Many phrases consisting of a verb and either an adverb or a preposition have meanings of their own not easily deduced from the separate meanings of the two words used in the phrase. So we use the phrase *to give up* in the sense of *to cease*, e.g. "I must *give up* smoking", without intending any idea of *giving* or *upward* direction.

In some cases the meaning of at least one of the words used is still apparent in the meaning of the phrase, e.g. "I shall *write up* a full account", where the word *write* still means what it says, but the word *up* means *completely*.

In some cases the same phrase may have two meanings, e.g. "You *take on* (i.e. undertake) too much." "Don't *take on* so (i.e. take offence so easily)."

Sometimes a phrase of this kind is simply metaphorical, e.g. "I confessed because I was *leant on*" (i.e. subjected to threats).

Some such phrasal verbs may include more than one adverb or preposition, e.g. "I can't *put up with* (i.e. suffer) this noise."

Some verbs, especially one-syllable verbs, are used in this way with a great variety of adverb or preposition particles, as they are called.

Exercises on phrasal verbs

1. Write sentences using each of these verbs with the adverb particle *up* in such a way as to show the meaning of the phrase as a phrasal verb.

   back, bring, buck, do, get, give, lay, let, look, make, put, set, turn.

2. Write sentences showing the meaning of the phrasal verbs formed by adding the particles shown to the following verbs:

break –	*down, into, off, out*		go –	*against, ahead,*
bring –	*about, in, off, on,*			*along with, at, by, for,*
	round, to			*on, on about, over, with*
call –	*off, on, out*		keep –	*back, in with, on, on at*
carry –	*off, on, out*		knock –	*about, back, down, off*
come –	*about, across, by, in for,*		lay –	*in, into, off, on*
	into, of, off, round, to,		look –	*after, out*
	upon		make –	*for, off, out, up for*
do –	*away with, down, for,*		put –	*off, on, out, up with*
	in, out of, without		set –	*in, off, out*
get –	*about, around, at, on,*		stand –	*by, for, in, out, up for*
	on to, over, up to		take –	*after, in, off, on, to, up*
give –	*away, in, out, over*		turn –	*down, in, on, out, to*